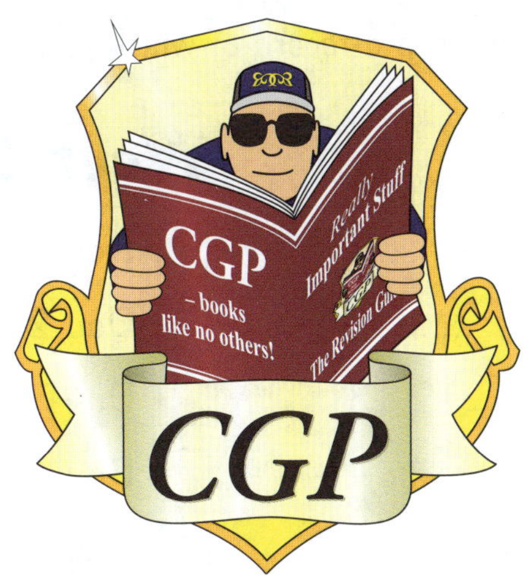

Supercharge your skills this summer!

KS1 Mental Maths might seem a bit daunting, but this smashing book from CGP is just the thing to get pupils' skills multiplying.

It's sure to build up their confidence, with a marvellous activity every single day of the term, and a whole range of Mental Maths skills covered.

And that's not all — colourful pictures and helpful examples are all included too. Let the good times (tables) roll!

What CGP is all about

Our sole aim here at CGP is to produce the highest quality books — carefully written, immaculately presented and dangerously close to being funny.

Then we work our socks off to get them out to you — at the cheapest possible prices.

Contents

Published by CGP

ISBN: 978 1 78908 765 9

Editors: Emma Clayton, Eleanor Crabtree, Camilla Sheridan, Charlotte Sheridan, George Wright

With thanks to Sharon Gulliver and Glenn Rogers for the proofreading.

With thanks to Emily Smith for the copyright research.

Cover and graphics used throughout the book © www.edu-clips.com
Clipart from Corel®

Coin images used on page 34: 5 and 50 pence coins © iStock.com/duncan1890, 10 pence coins © iStock.com/john shepherd, 20 pence coins © iStock.com/Jaap2, 2 pence coins © iStock.com/peterspiro, 1 penny coins © iStock.com/coopder1

Printed by Zenith Print & Packaging Ltd, Pontypridd.
Based on the classic CGP style created by Richard Parsons.

How to Use this Book

- This book contains <u>60 daily practice tests</u>.

- We've split them into <u>12 sections</u> — that's roughly one for <u>each week</u> of the Year 1 <u>summer term</u>.

- Each week is made up of <u>5 tests</u>, so there's one for <u>every school day</u> of the term (Monday – Friday).

- Each test should take about <u>10 minutes</u> to complete.

- Pupils should aim to do their <u>working in their heads</u>, without writing it down.

- The tests contain a <u>mix</u> of mental maths topics from <u>Year 1</u>. <u>New Year 1 topics</u> are gradually introduced as you go through the book.

- The tests <u>increase in difficulty</u> as you progress through the term.

- Each test looks something like this:

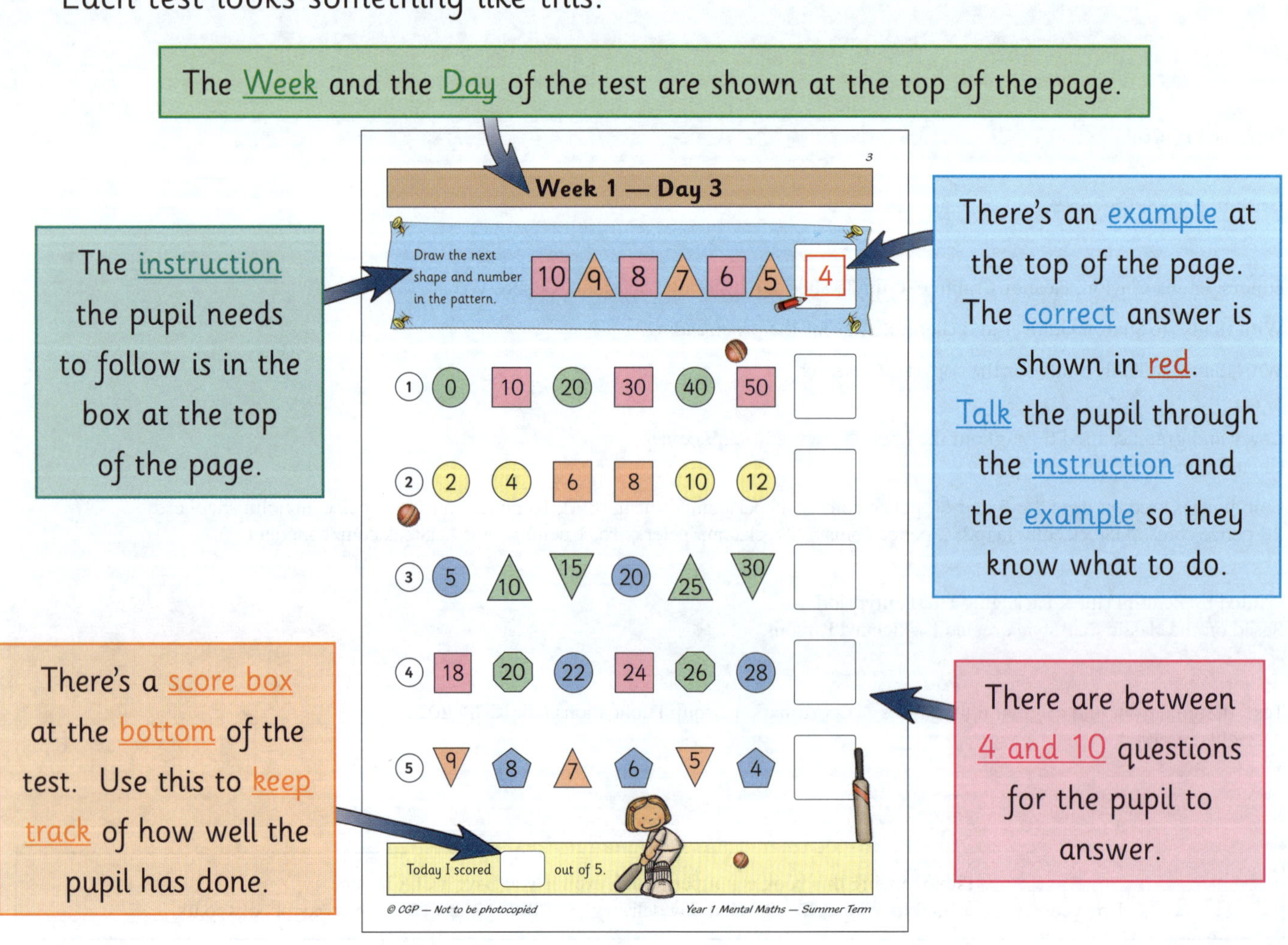

Week 1 — Day 1

1. 5 — 15, 10, 14

5. 19 — 11, 1, 9

2. 3 — 17, 3, 13

6. 14 — 6, 16, 4

3. 7 — 19, 13, 10

7. 18 — 2, 7, 4

4. 10 — 10, 11, 1

8. 9 — 11, 1, 19

Today I scored ☐ out of 8.

Year 1 Mental Maths — Summer Term

Week 1 — Day 2

Write the answer.
Use the pictures
to help you.

$3 \times 2 = \boxed{6}$

1   

$2 \times 2 = \boxed{}$

2

$4 \times 2 = \boxed{}$

3

$1 \times 2 = \boxed{}$

4 

$5 \times 2 = \boxed{}$

5 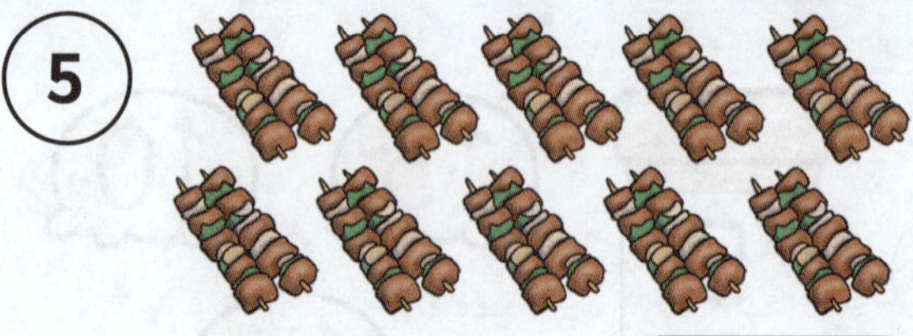

$10 \times 2 = \boxed{}$

6 

$6 \times 2 = \boxed{}$

7 

$7 \times 2 = \boxed{}$

8 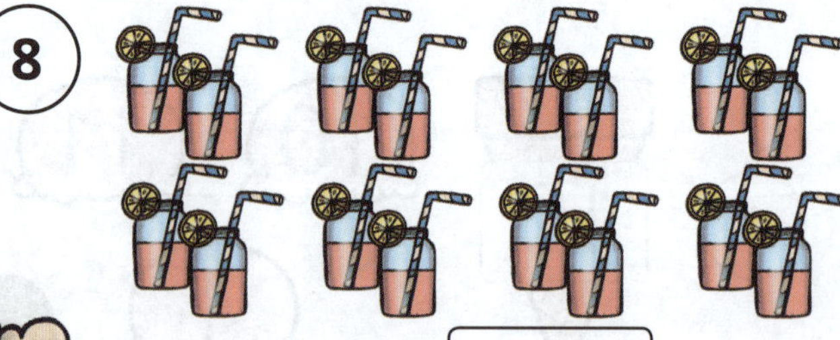

$8 \times 2 = \boxed{}$

Today I scored $\boxed{}$ out of 8.

Week 1 — Day 3

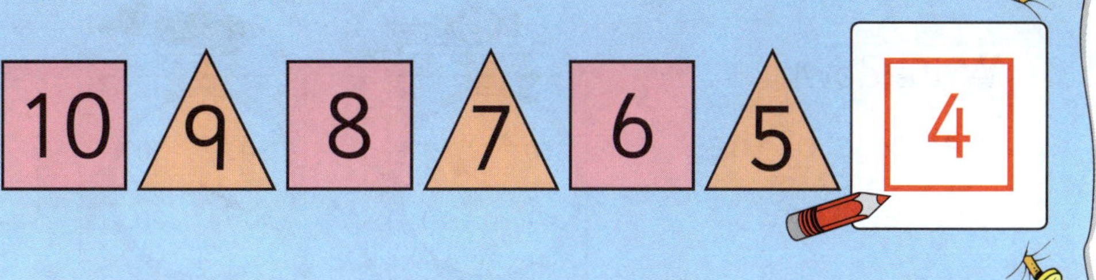

1.  0 10 20 30 40 50

2. 2 4 6 8 10 12

3. 5 10 15 20 25 30

4. 18 20 22 24 26 28

5.  9 8 7 6 5 4 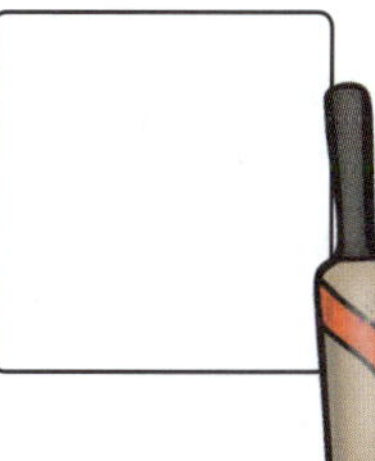

Today I scored [ ] out of 5.

   Year 1 Mental Maths — Summer Term

Week 1 — Day 4

Week 1 — Day 5

The coach needs to split the players into two equal teams. How many players will there be in each team?

1 

2 

3 

4 

5 

Today I scored ☐ out of 5.

Year 1 Mental Maths — Summer Term

Week 2 — Day 1

Fill in the missing number. Use the pictures to help you.

$6 \times 2 = 12$

1 

$\boxed{} \times 2 = 8$

2

$\boxed{} \times 2 = 2$

3 

$\boxed{} \times 2 = 6$

4 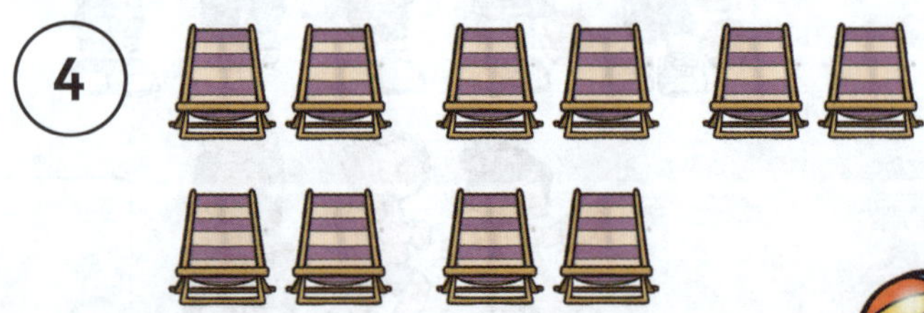

$\boxed{} \times 2 = 10$

5 

$\boxed{} \times 2 = 16$

6 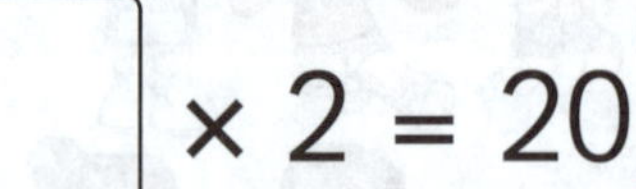

$\boxed{} \times 2 = 20$

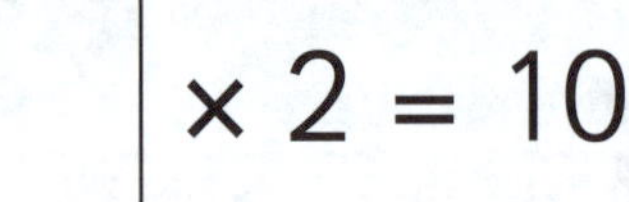

Today I scored $\boxed{}$ out of 6.

Week 2 — Day 2

Circle the name of the shape that there are more of.

square
circle

1
triangle
circle

2
triangle
rectangle

3
square
circle

4
triangle
square

5
rectangle
square

Today I scored out of 5.

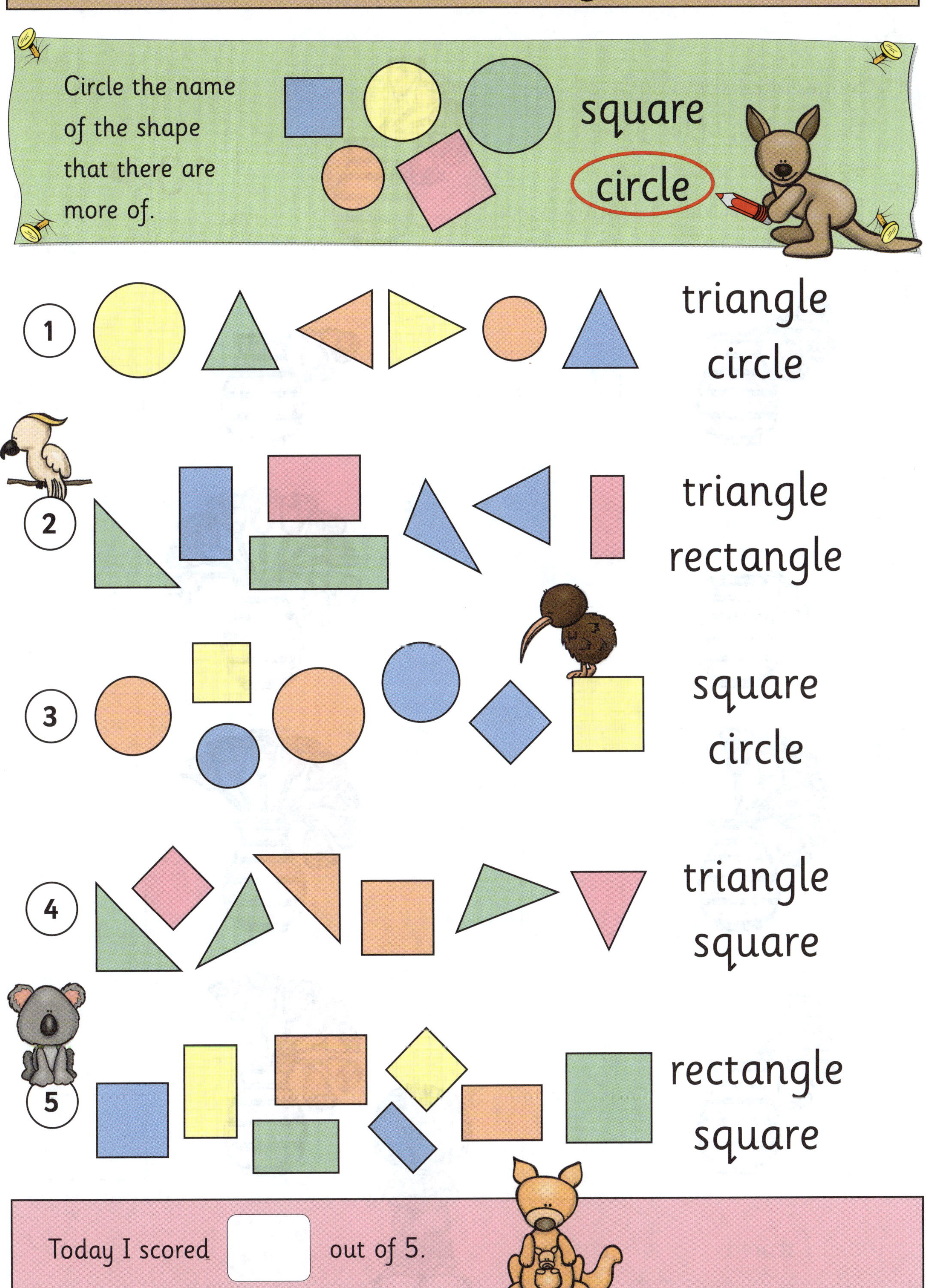

Week 2 — Day 3

Samuel has some flowers.
He puts half of the flowers
in the vase. How many
flowers were there in total?

10

1

2

3

4

5

6

7

8

Today I scored ___ out of 8.

Week 2 — Day 4

The puppies are split into two equal groups. Fill in the missing numbers in the division.

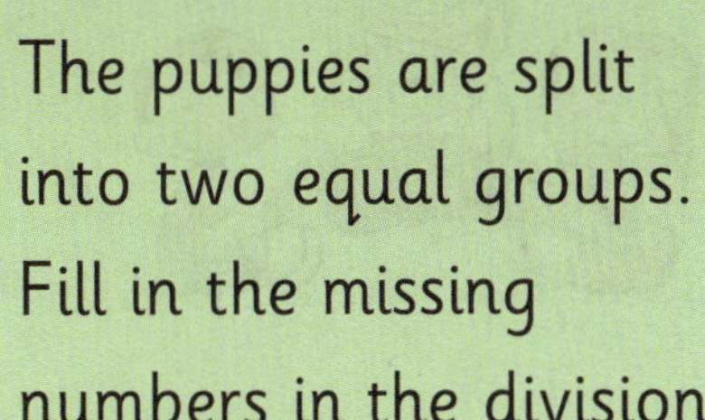

$$6 \div 2 = 3$$

1 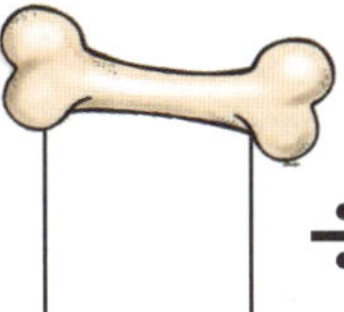

$$\boxed{} \div 2 = \boxed{}$$

2 

$$\boxed{} \div 2 = \boxed{}$$

3 

$$\boxed{} \div 2 = \boxed{}$$

4 

$$\boxed{} \div 2 = \boxed{}$$

Today I scored $\boxed{}$ out of 4.

Week 2 — Day 5

Fill in the missing number.

$\boxed{10} - 4 = 6$

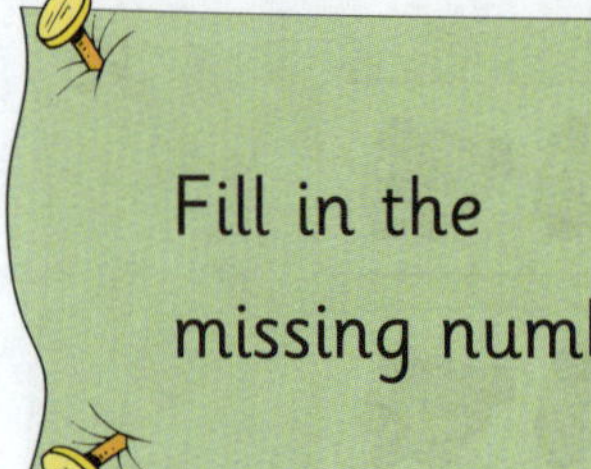

1. $\boxed{} - 2 = 4$

2. $\boxed{} + 3 = 7$

3. $\boxed{} + 8 = 9$

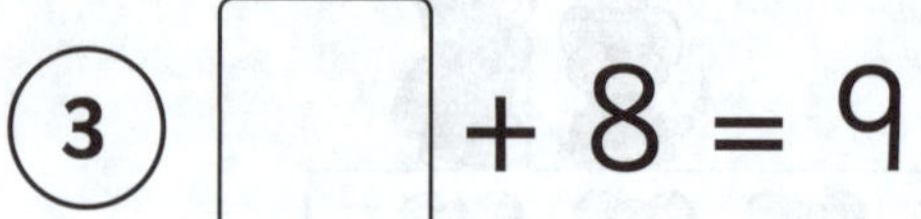

4. $\boxed{} - 4 = 4$

5. $\boxed{} + 6 = 12$

6. $\boxed{} - 2 = 17$

7. $\boxed{} - 8 = 12$

8. $\boxed{} + 5 = 16$

9. $\boxed{} - 10 = 8$

10. $\boxed{} - 5 = 6$

Today I scored $\boxed{}$ out of 10.

Week 3 — Day 1

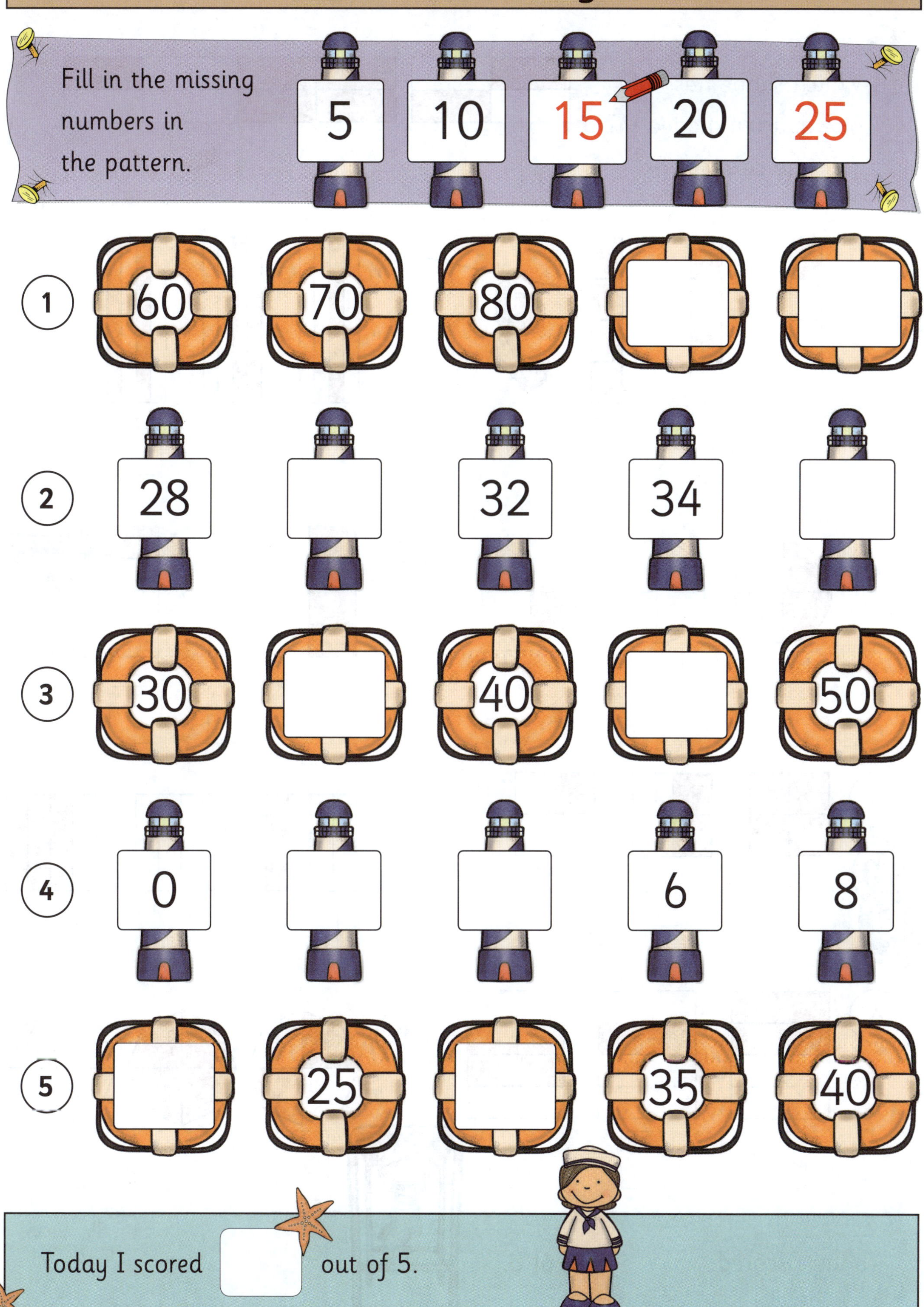

Year 1 Mental Maths — Summer Term

Week 3 — Day 2

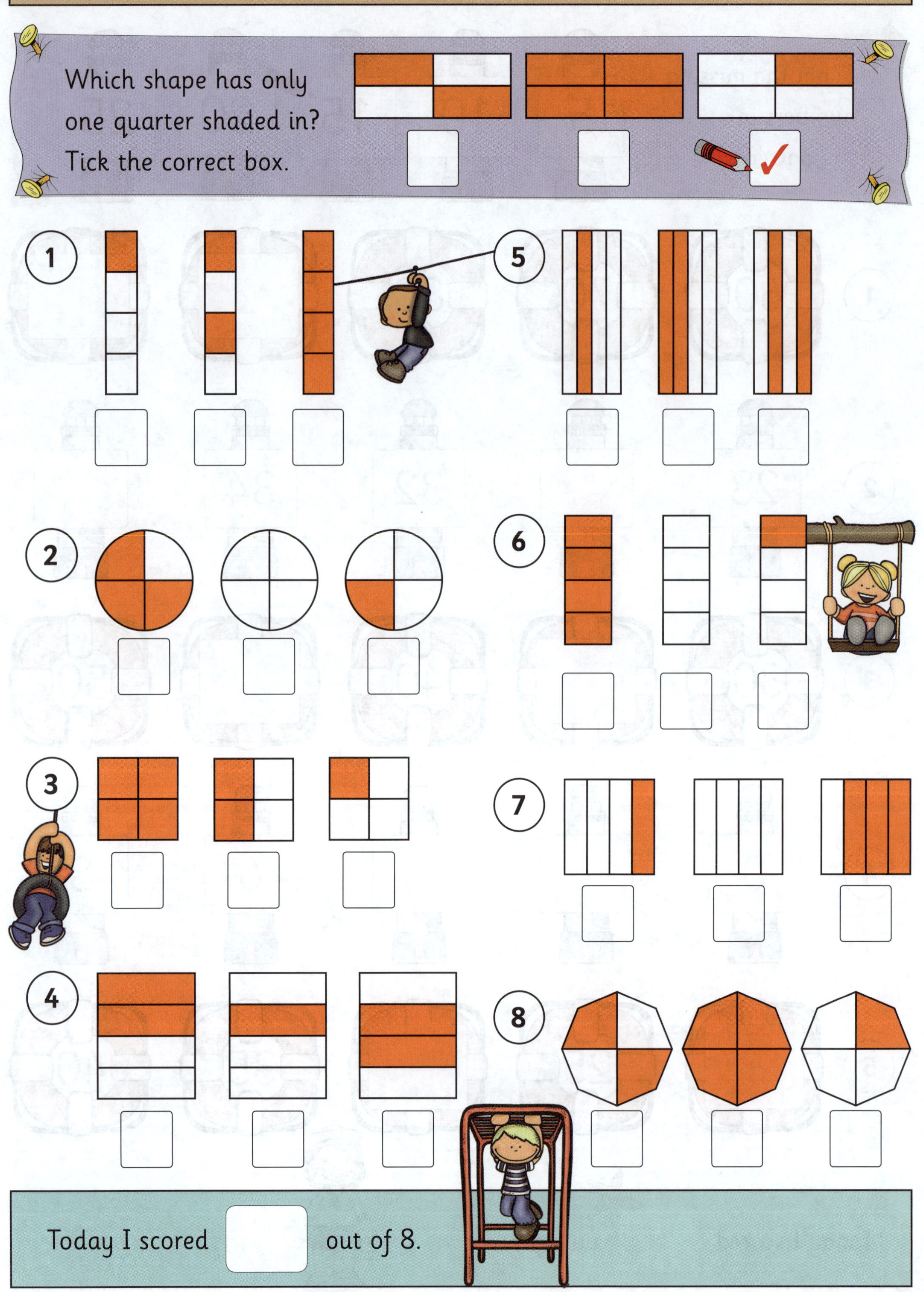

Which shape has only one quarter shaded in? Tick the correct box.
1
2
3
4
5
6
7
8
Today I scored   out of 8.

Week 3 — Day 3

Fill in the missing numbers. Use the pictures to help you.

$$2 \times \boxed{5} = 10$$

1 

$$1 \times \boxed{} = 5$$

2 

$$3 \times \boxed{} = 6$$

3 

$$4 \times \boxed{} = 8$$

4 

$$6 \times \boxed{} = 12$$

5 

$$5 \times \boxed{} = 25$$

6

$$3 \times \boxed{} = 15$$

7 

$$5 \times \boxed{} = 10$$

Today I scored $\boxed{}$ out of 7.

Year 1 Mental Maths — Summer Term

Week 3 — Day 4

The two birds want to share the worms between them equally. How many worms will each bird get?

1

2

3

4

5

6

7

8

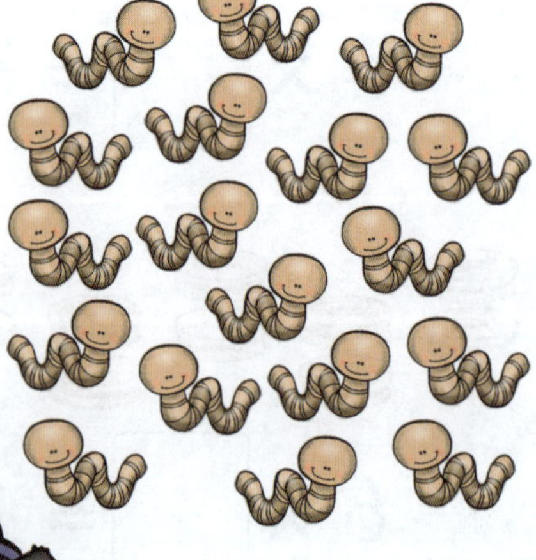

Today I scored ☐ out of 8.

Week 3 — Day 5

Fill in the missing number.

$16 + 3 = 19$ 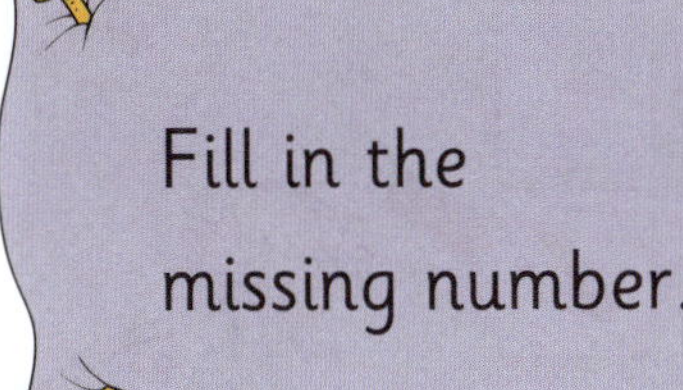

1. $\boxed{} - 6 = 4$

2. $12 - 6 = \boxed{}$

3. $\boxed{} + 4 = 7$

4. $13 - \boxed{} = 11$

5. $17 - \boxed{} = 11$

6. $\boxed{} + 4 = 9$

7. $18 - \boxed{} = 10$

8. $\boxed{} - 5 = 9$

9. $20 - \boxed{} = 7$

10. $16 - \boxed{} = 4$

Today I scored $\boxed{}$ out of 10.

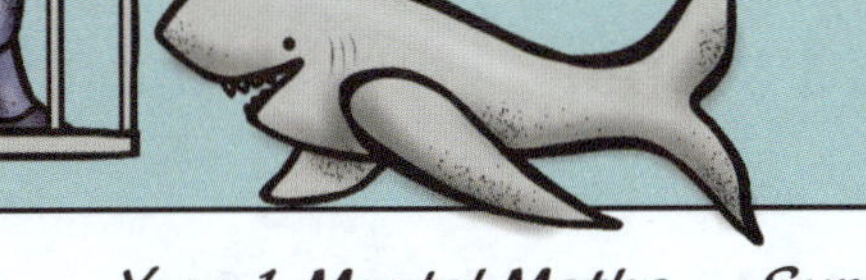

Year 1 Mental Maths — Summer Term

Week 4 — Day 1

Tick the name of the shape that there are most of.

cuboid ☐
sphere ✓
pyramid ☐

1
pyramid ☐
sphere ☐
cube ☐

2
pyramid ☐
sphere ☐
cuboid ☐

3
cube ☐
sphere ☐
pyramid ☐

4
pyramid ☐
sphere ☐
cube ☐

5
pyramid ☐
sphere ☐
cuboid ☐

6
pyramid ☐
sphere ☐
cube ☐

Today I scored ☐ out of 6.

Week 4 — Day 2

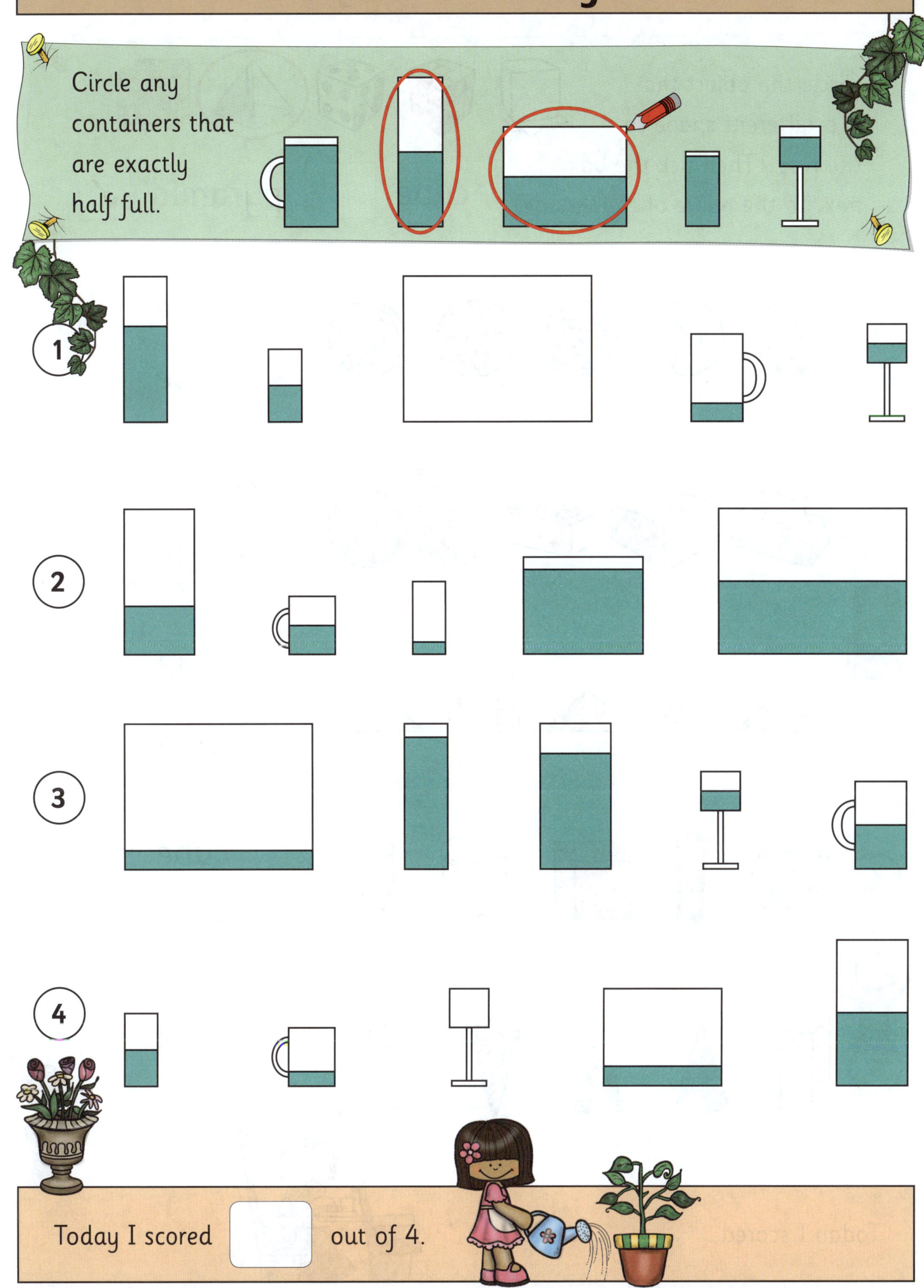

    Year 1 Mental Maths — Summer Term

Week 4 — Day 3

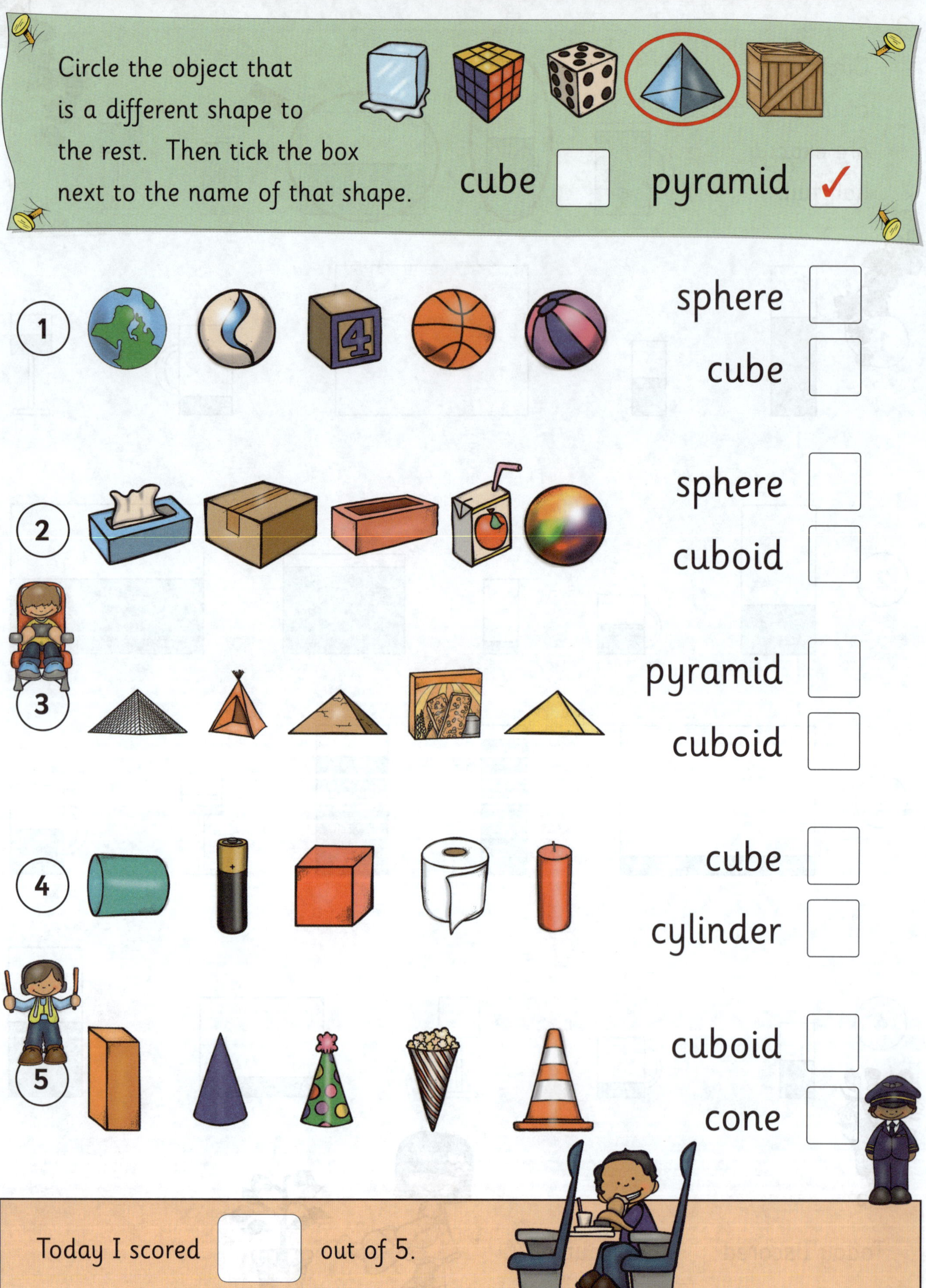

Circle the object that is a different shape to the rest. Then tick the box next to the name of that shape.

cube ☐   pyramid ✓

1. sphere ☐   cube ☐

2. sphere ☐   cuboid ☐

3. pyramid ☐   cuboid ☐

4. cube ☐   cylinder ☐

5. cuboid ☐   cone ☐

Today I scored ☐ out of 5.

Week 4 — Day 4

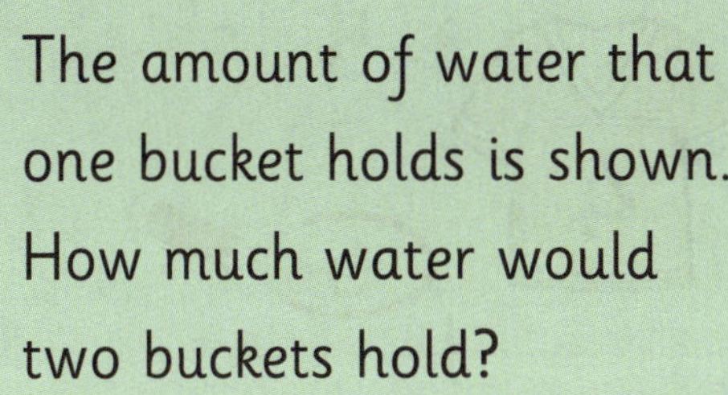

The amount of water that one bucket holds is shown. How much water would two buckets hold?

5 litres

10 litres

 **1**  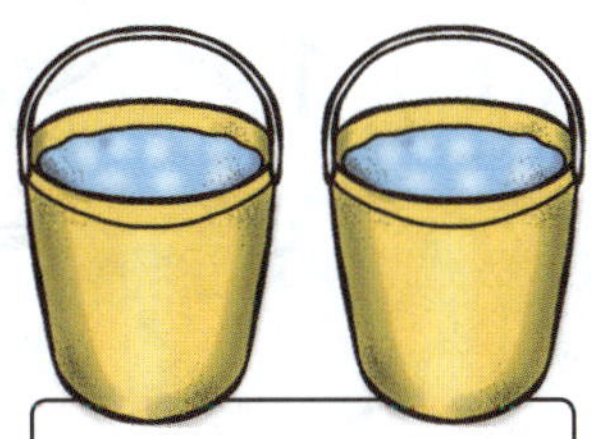

4 litres   litres

 **5** 

7 litres   litres

 **2**  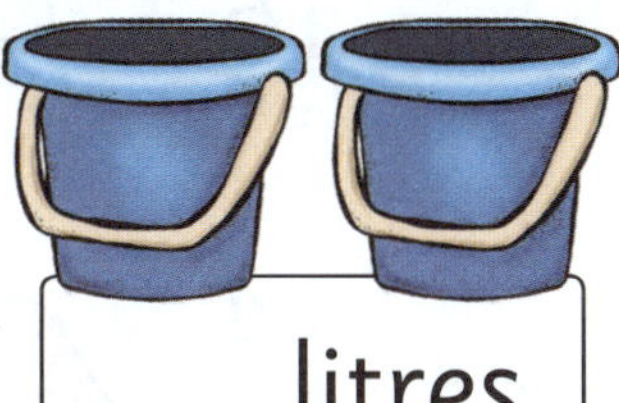

3 litres   litres

 **6** 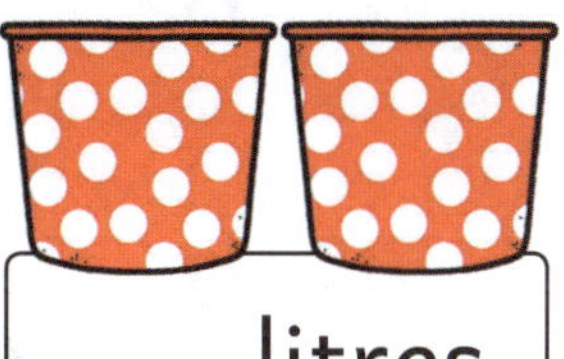

9 litres   litres

 **3**  

1 litre   litres

 **7** 

8 litres   litres

4  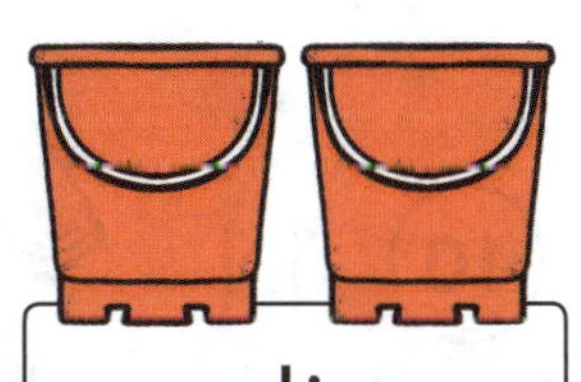

2 litres   litres

 **8** 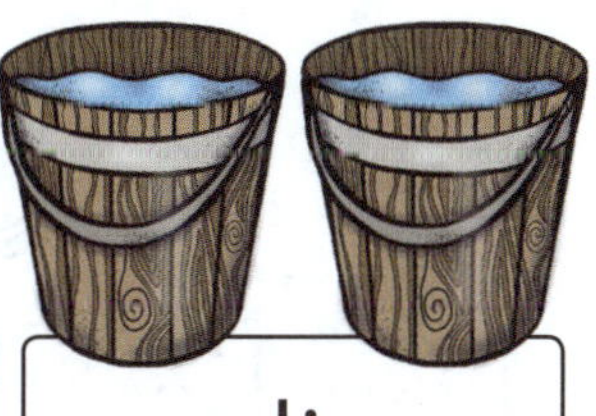

10 litres   litres

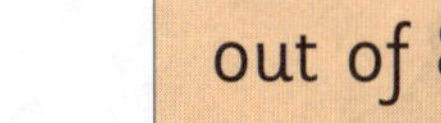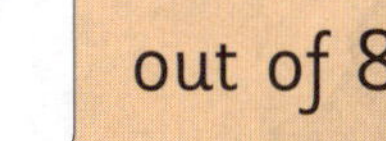

Today I scored ☐ out of 8.

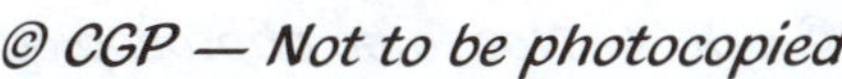

Year 1 Mental Maths — Summer Term

Week 4 — Day 5

Circle the pair of numbers with a difference equal to the number shown on the shirt.

Example shirt (4):
10, 4, 7 | 5, 7, 6

1.
7, 4, 8 | **[2]** | 2, 7, 3

2.
1, 4, 6 | **[6]** | 3, 7, 2

3.
8, 5, 6 | **[5]** | 2, 1, 4

4.
4, 1, 6 | **[9]** | 11, 3, 10

5.
10, 8, 12 | **[3]** | 15, 6, 2

6.
11, 12, 6 | **[10]** | 17, 16, 3

7.
20, 18, 16 | **[12]** | 19, 5, 4

8.
14, 3, 8 | **[8]** | 17, 16, 1

9.
17, 9, 6 | **[7]** | 15, 7, 13

10.
1, 11, 2 | **[18]** | 9, 19, 17

Today I scored ☐ out of 10.

Week 5 — Day 1

How many books are above
the plant on the shelves?
How many books are below it?

4 above

2 below

1

above

below

2

above

below

3

above

below

4

above

below

5

above

below

Today I scored ___ out of 5.

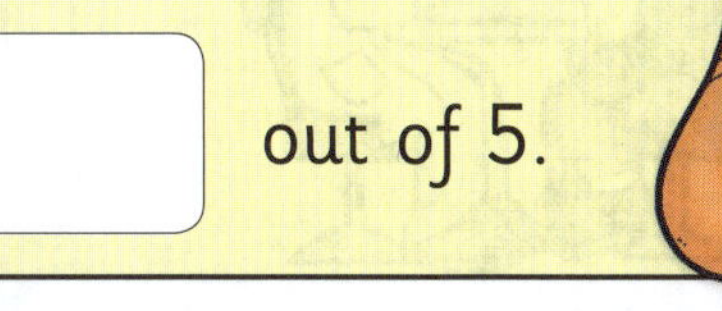
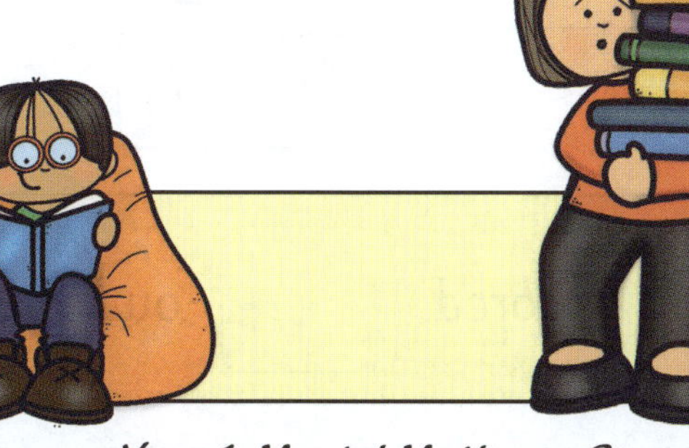

Year 1 Mental Maths — Summer Term

Week 5 — Day 2

Circle the calculation that is equal to the number shown.

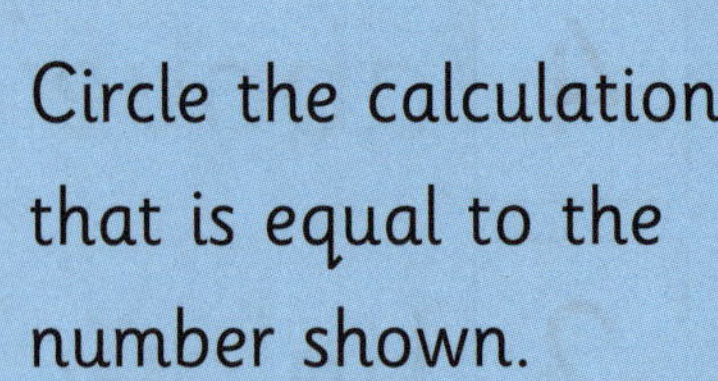

4

9 − 7
8 − 4
1 + 2

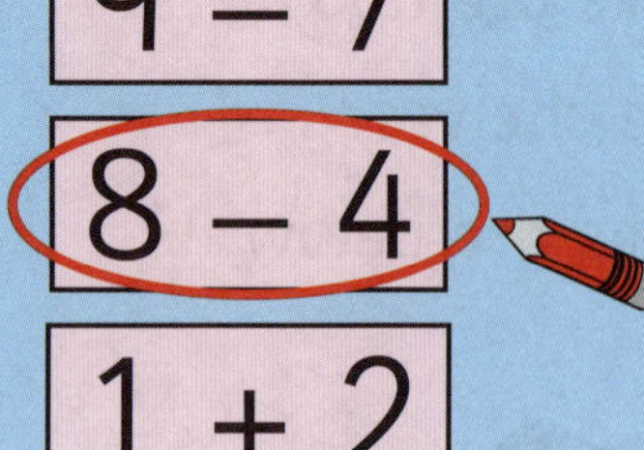

1   6

3 + 4
10 − 8
9 − 3

2   9

3 + 7
4 + 4
11 − 2

3   7

9 − 5
2 + 5
14 − 5

4   15

4 + 12
7 + 7
9 + 6

5   10

4 + 9
5 + 5
14 − 2

6   18

17 − 2
9 + 9
14 − 4

7   13

7 + 8
19 − 14
6 + 7

8   5

11 − 7
16 − 11
19 − 15

Today I scored ☐ out of 8.

Week 5 — Day 3

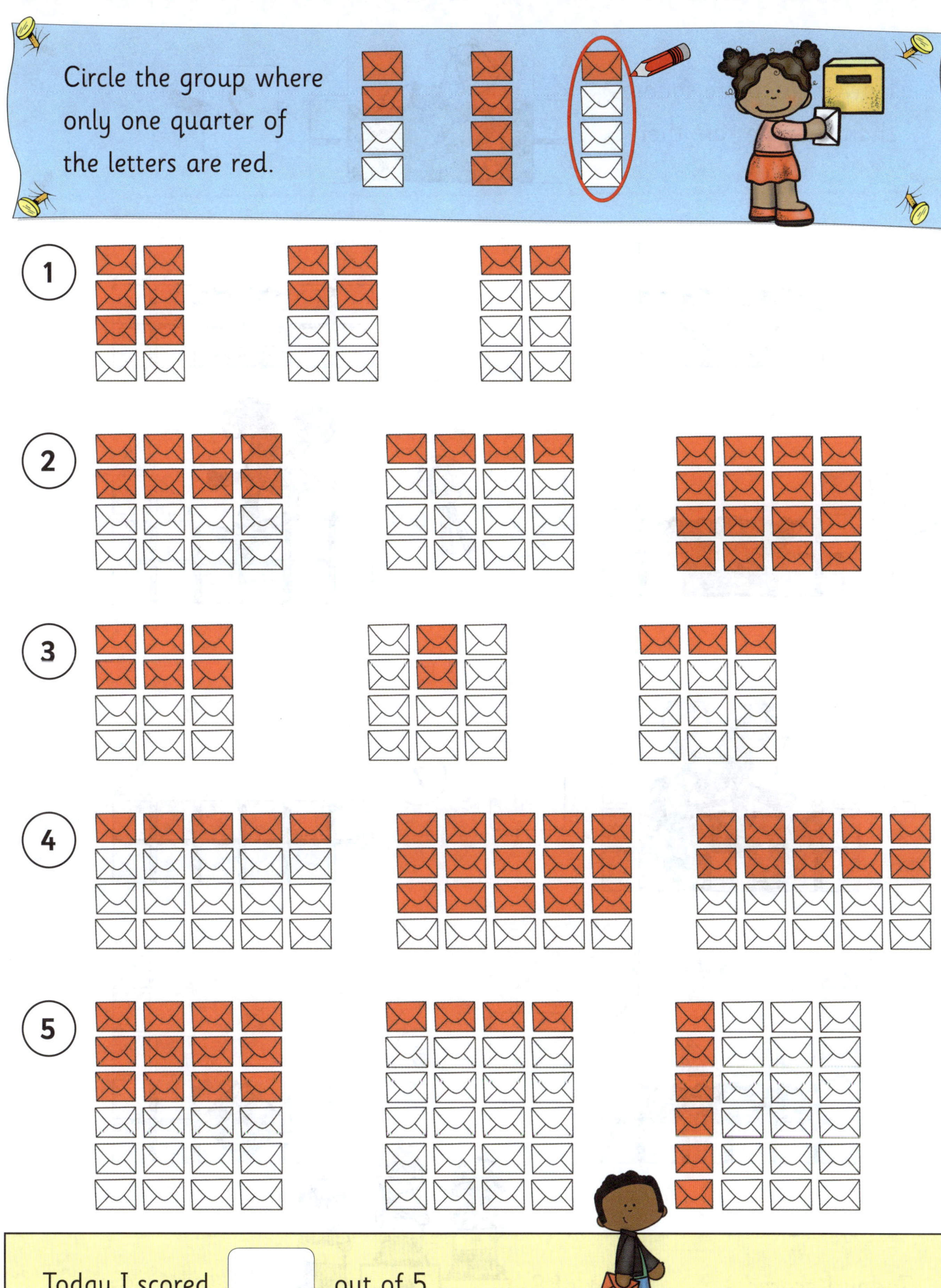

Circle the group where only one quarter of the letters are red.

1

2

3

4

5

Today I scored ⬚ out of 5.

Week 5 — Day 4

Today I scored ☐ out of 8.

Week 5 — Day 5

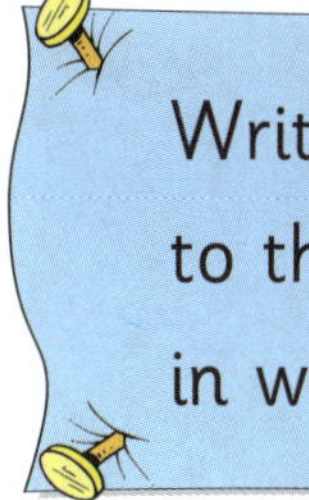 Write the answer to the calculation in words.

 1 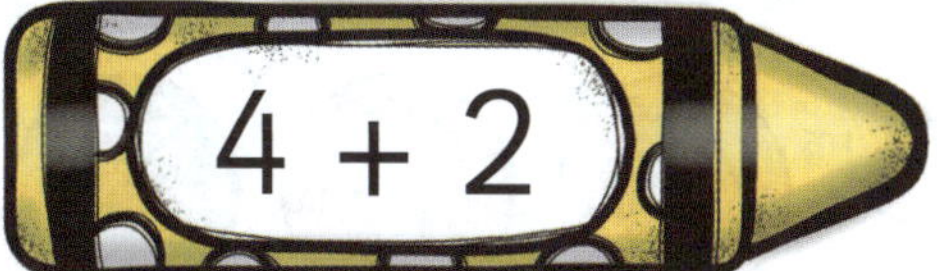

 2 

 3 

 4 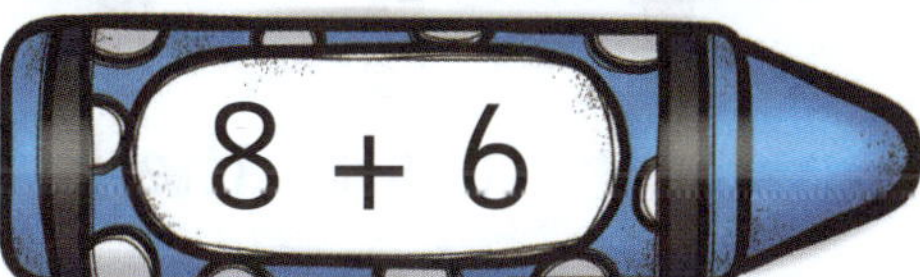

 5 

 6 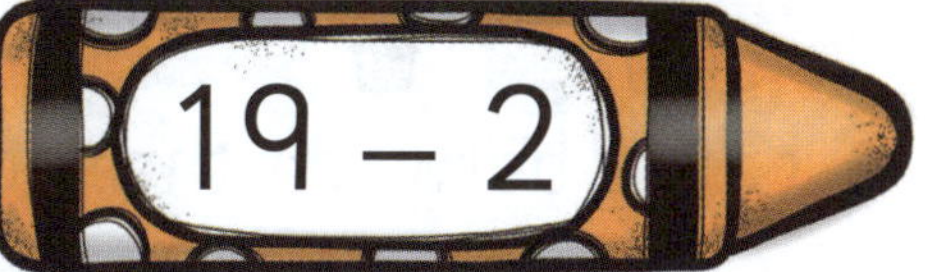

 7 

 8 

Today I scored [ ] out of 8.

Year 1 Mental Maths — Summer Term

Week 6 — Day 1

Circle the shape that is being described.

It is between the circle and the square.

---

1 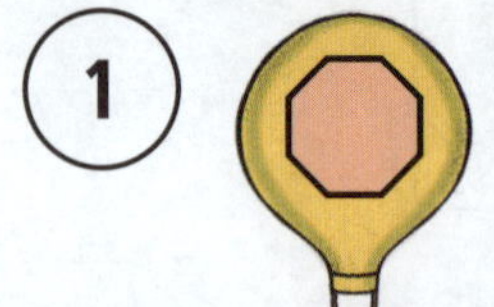

It is between the square and the triangle.

5 

It is to the right of the triangle.

---

2 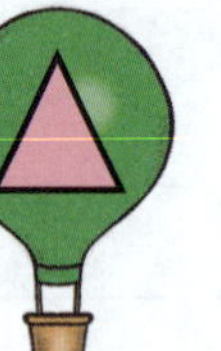

It is between the rectangle and the circle.

6 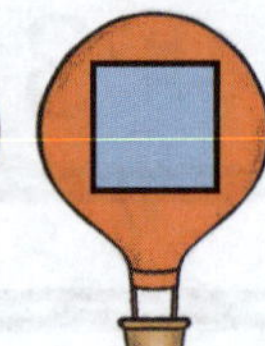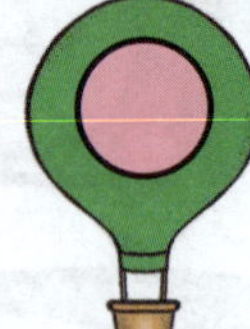

It is to the left of the square.

---

3 

It is next to the rectangle.

7 

It is between the rectangle and the circle.

---

4 

It is between the rectangle and the triangle.

8 

It is to the right of the circle.

Today I scored ⬚ out of 8.

Week 6 — Day 2

Which letter will the arrow on the compass point to after the turn?

A whole turn

 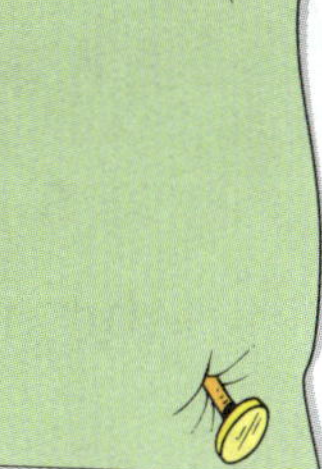

N

1 

A half turn

5

A quarter turn clockwise

2

A quarter turn clockwise

6

A three-quarter turn clockwise

3

A whole turn

7

A half turn

4

A half turn

8

A quarter turn clockwise

Today I scored ____ out of 8.

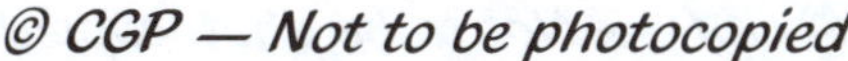

Year 1 Mental Maths — Summer Term

Week 6 — Day 3

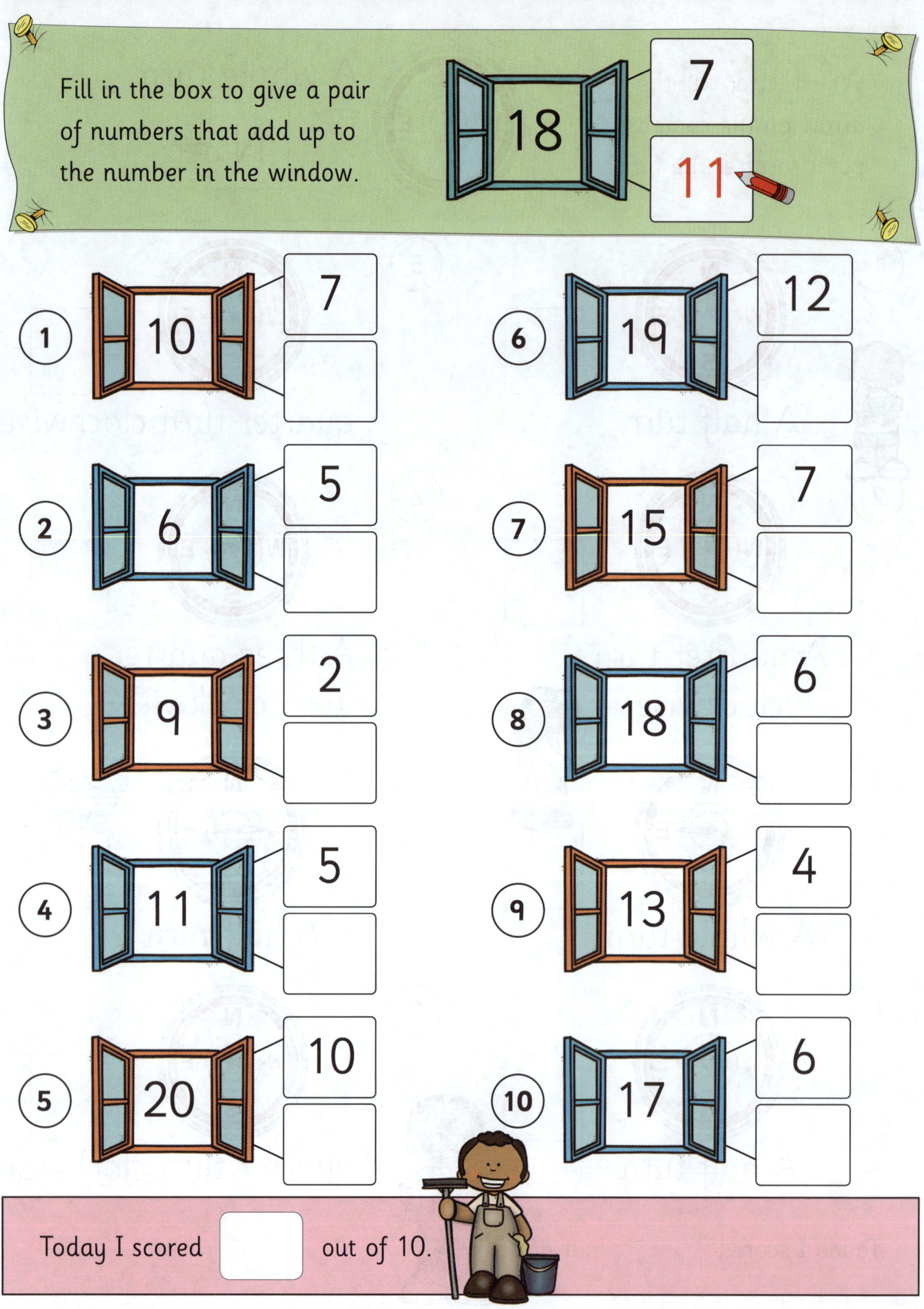

Today I scored ☐ out of 10.

Week 6 — Day 4

Write a number in the box to complete the sentence.

Sam has won 8 games.
Dev has won 4 more.

Dev has won **12** games.

1. Joe has won 8 games.
Sue has won 4 fewer.

Sue has won ☐ games.

2. Rani has won 6 games.
Li has won half as many.

Li has won ☐ games.

3. Mim has won 5 games.
Talia has won 7 more.

Talia has won ☐ games.

4. Leo has won 11 games.
Lara has won 8 fewer.

Lara has won ☐ games.

5. Zahra has won 8 games.
Ed has won double this.

Ed has won ☐ games.

6. Ben has won 19 games.
Kat has won 14 fewer.

Kat has won ☐ games.

Today I scored ☐ out of 6.

Week 6 — Day 5

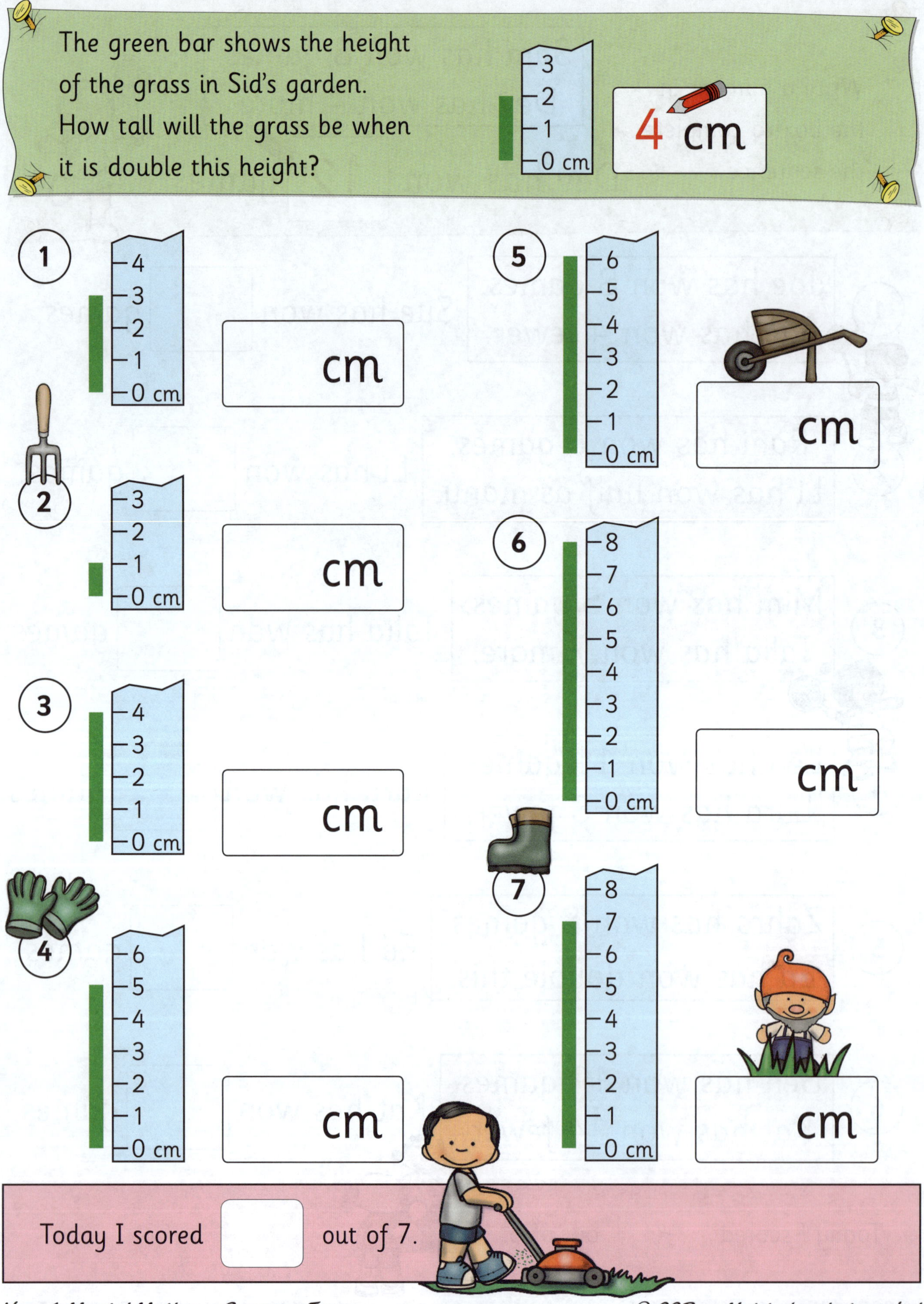

The green bar shows the height of the grass in Sid's garden. How tall will the grass be when it is double this height?
4 cm
1
cm
2
cm
3
cm
4
cm
5
cm
6
cm
7
cm
Today I scored ____ out of 7.

Week 7 — Day 1

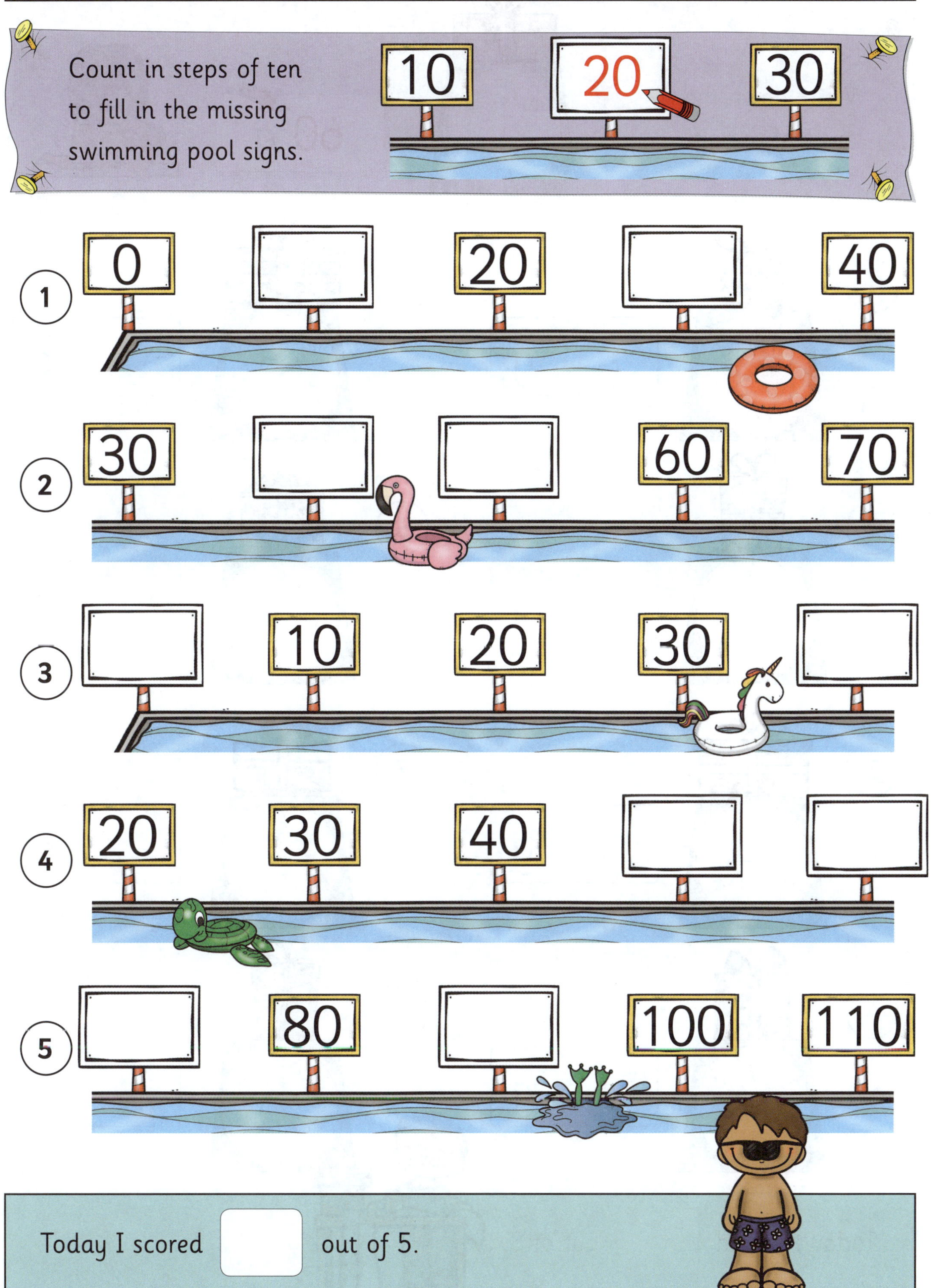

Today I scored ☐ out of 5.

Year 1 Mental Maths — Summer Term

Week 7 — Day 2

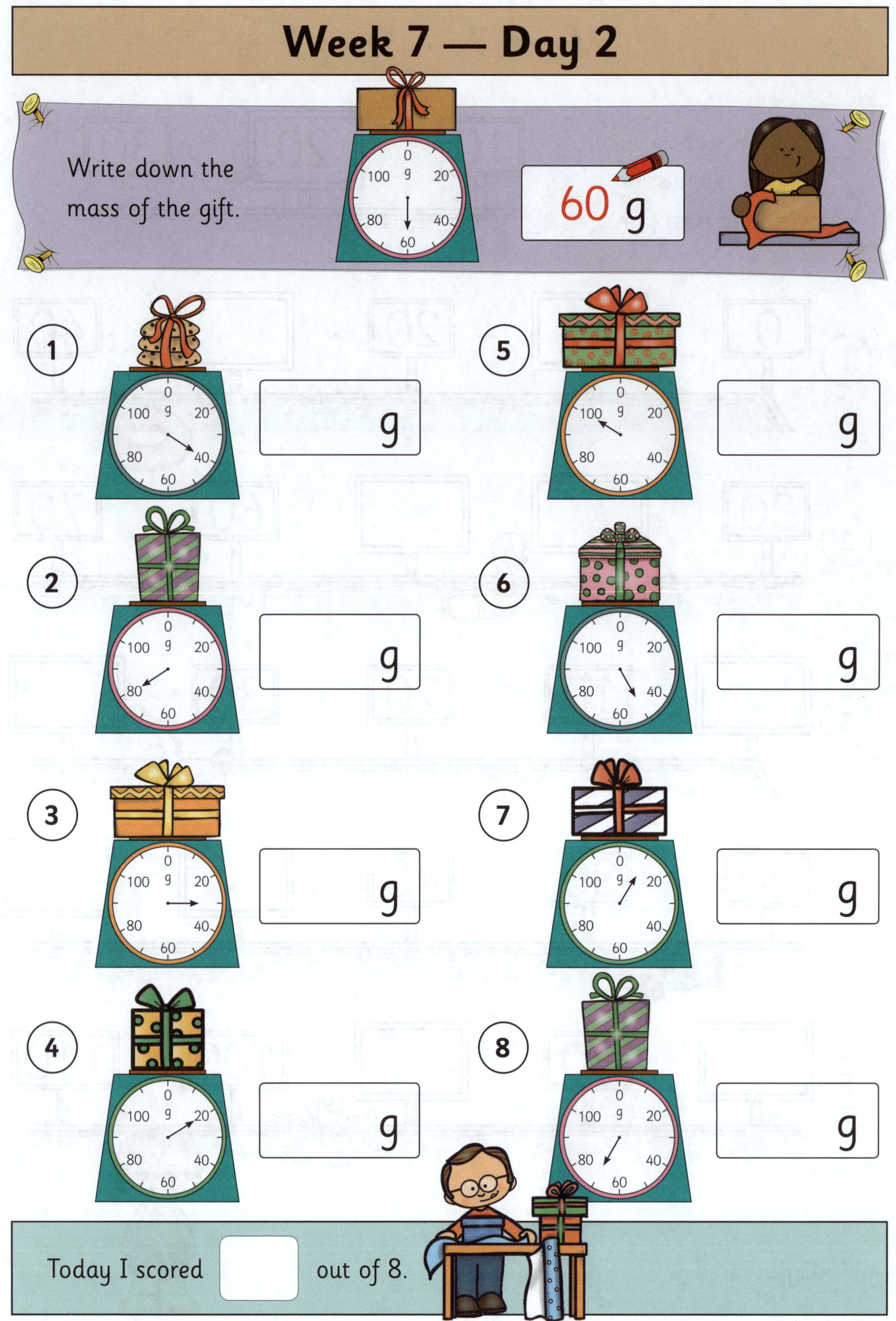

Write down the
mass of the gift.
0
g
100
20
80
40
60
60 g
1
0
g
100
20
80
40
60
g
5
0
g
100
20
80
40
60
g
2
0
g
100
20
80
40
60
g
6
0
g
100
20
80
40
60
g
3
0
g
100
20
80
40
60
g
7
0
g
100
20
80
40
60
g
4
0
g
100
20
80
40
60
g
8
0
g
100
20
80
40
60
g
Today I scored   out of 8.

Week 7 — Day 3

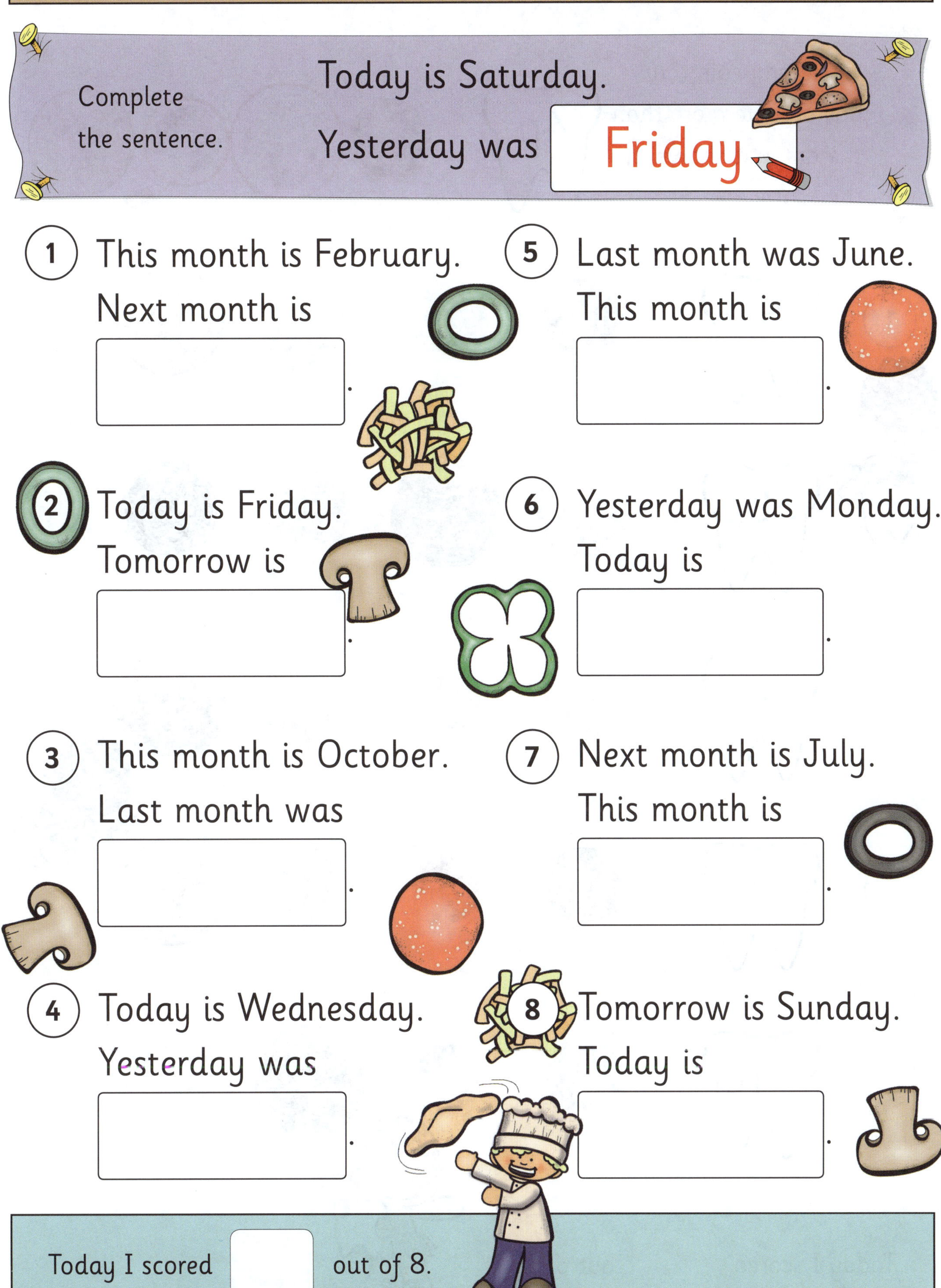

Complete the sentence.

Today is Saturday.

Yesterday was **Friday**.

1 This month is February.
Next month is

2 Today is Friday.
Tomorrow is

3 This month is October.
Last month was

4 Today is Wednesday.
Yesterday was

5 Last month was June.
This month is

6 Yesterday was Monday.
Today is

7 Next month is July.
This month is

8 Tomorrow is Sunday.
Today is

Today I scored [ ] out of 8.

Year 1 Mental Maths — Summer Term

Week 7 — Day 4

Circle any coin that has a value more than the amount shown on the tooth.

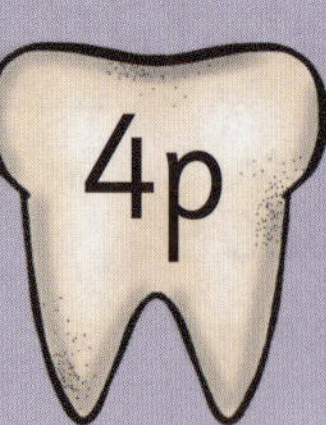 

1.  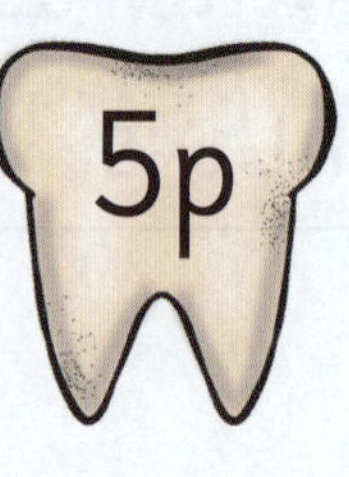 5p    

2. 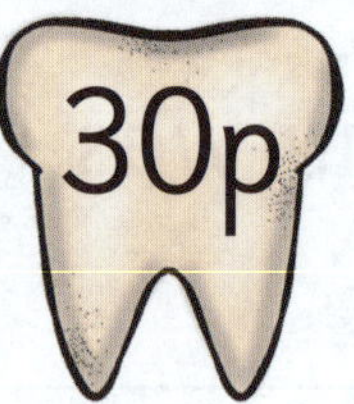 30p    

3.  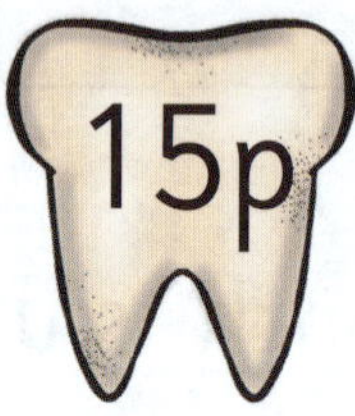 15p    

4.  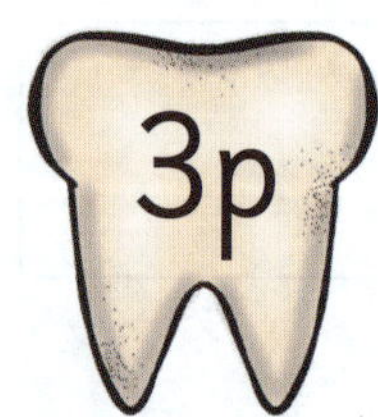 3p    

5. 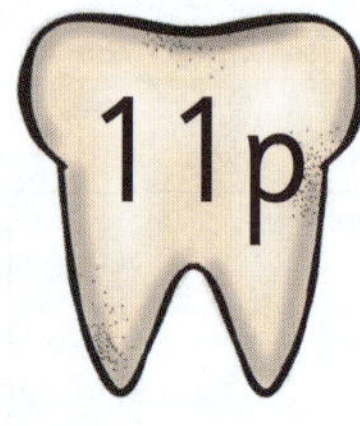 11p   

Today I scored ☐ out of 5.

Week 7 — Day 5

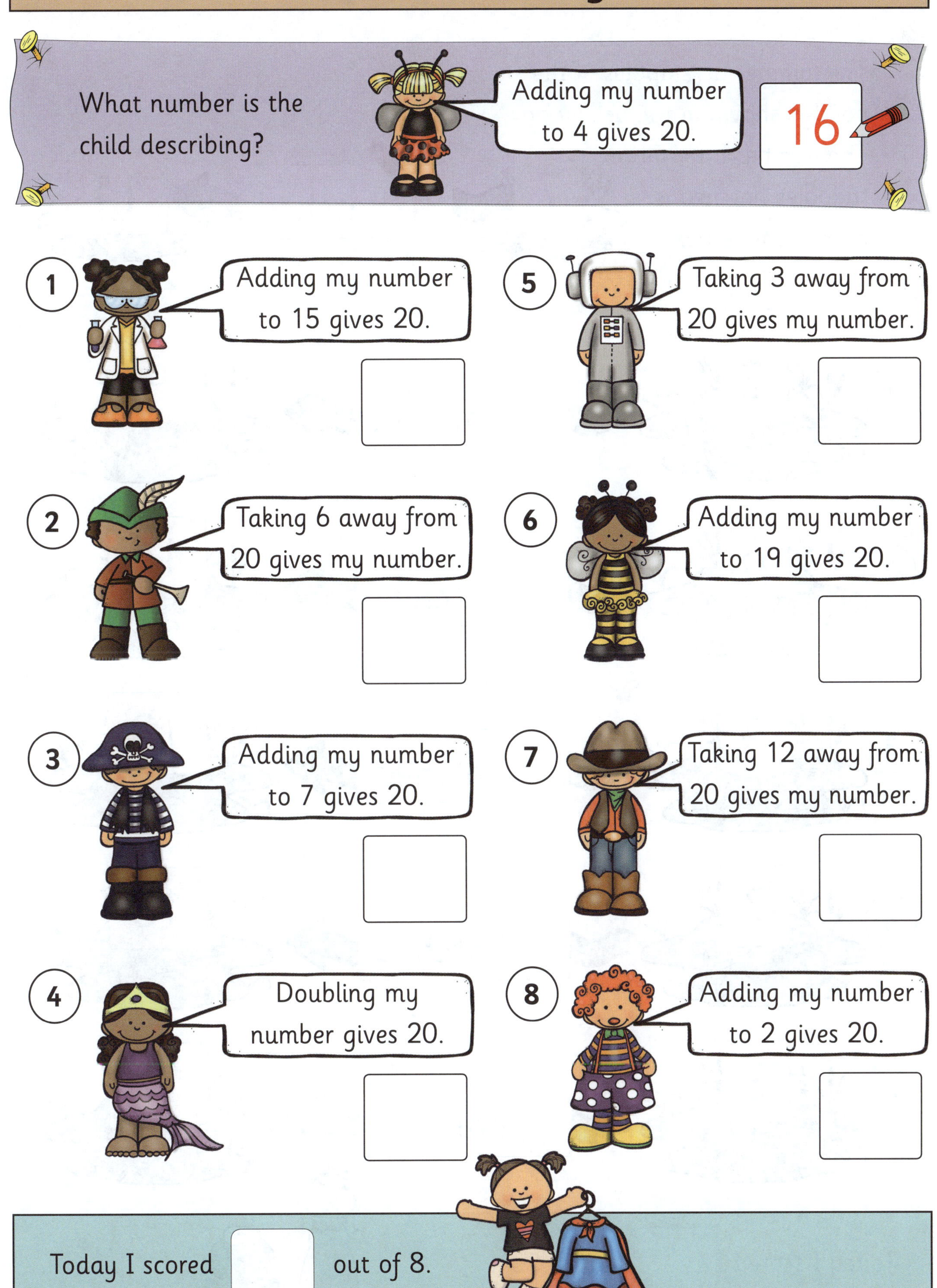

Year 1 Mental Maths — Summer Term

Week 8 — Day 1

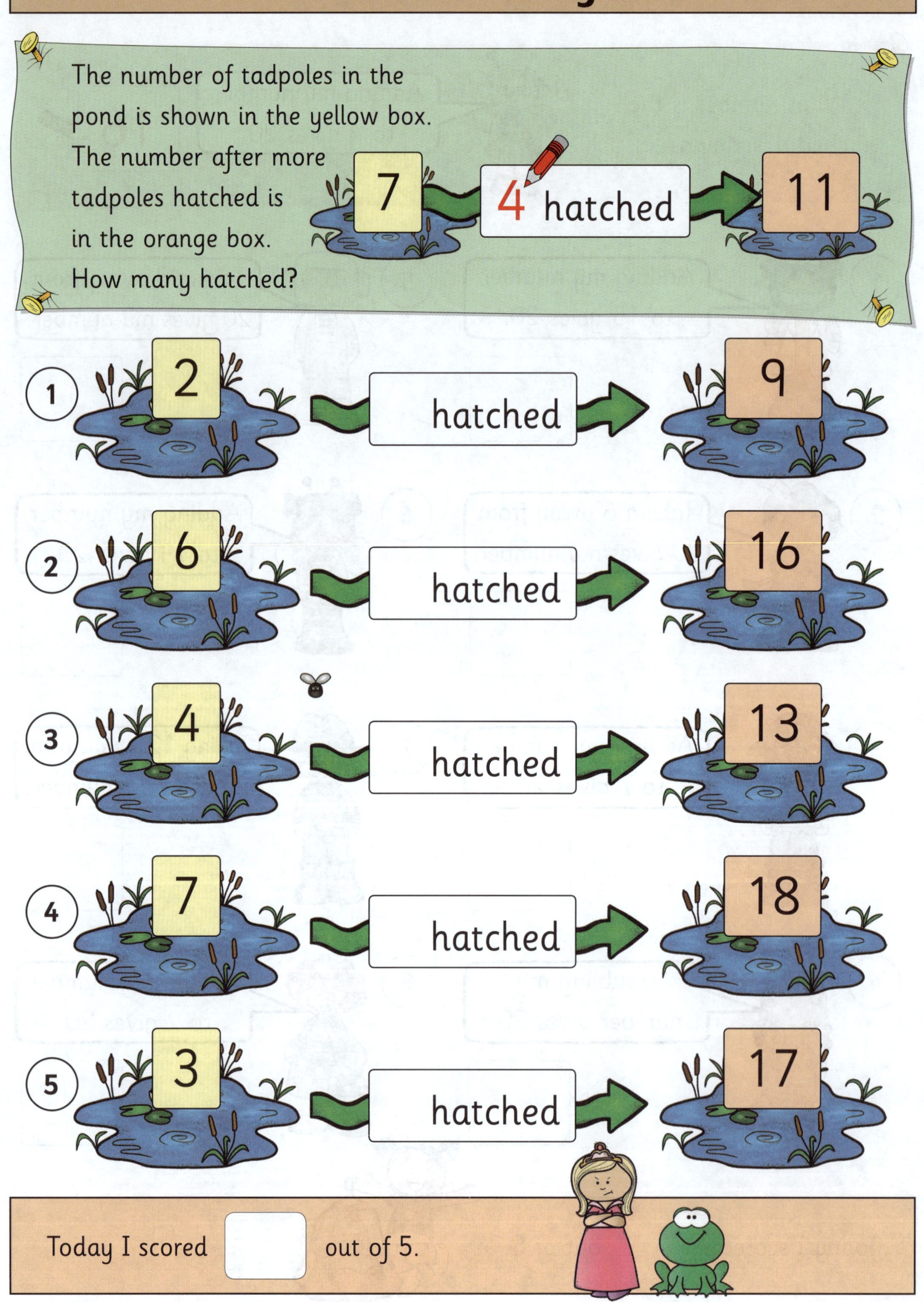

Today I scored ___ out of 5.

Week 8 — Day 2

The child says the time. Does the time match the clock that they are holding? Tick 'Yes' or 'No'.

1

Yes No

2

Yes No

3

Yes No

4

Yes No

5

Yes No

6

Yes No

Today I scored ___ out of 6.

Year 1 Mental Maths — Summer Term

Week 8 — Day 3

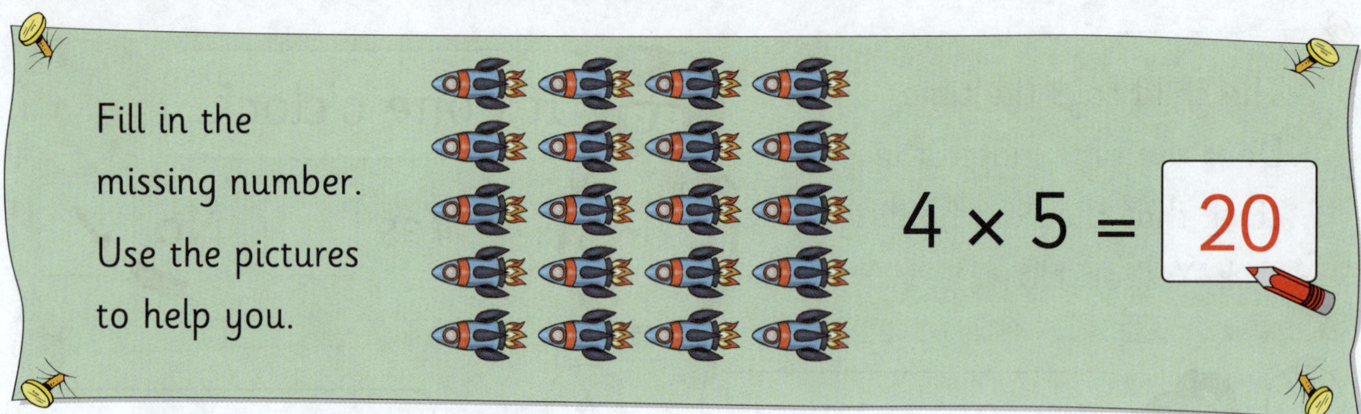

1  1 × 5 = ☐

2 3 × 5 = ☐

3  2 × 5 = ☐

4 5 × 5 = ☐

5 7 × 5 = ☐

Today I scored ☐ out of 5.

Week 8 — Day 4

Look at the clock. Circle the time it will be in one hour.

4 o'clock

6 o'clock

1

9 o'clock

8 o'clock

2

3 o'clock

5 o'clock

6

half past 3

half past 4

7

half past 9

half past 7

3

10 o'clock

11 o'clock

8

half past 11

half past 12

4

1 o'clock

2 o'clock

9

half past 12

half past 2

5

8 o'clock

10 o'clock

10

half past 5

half past 6

Today I scored ☐ out of 10.

Year 1 Mental Maths — Summer Term

Week 8 — Day 5

Circle the correct calculation.

11 + 7 = 17

12 + 4 = 16 (circled)

1) 13 + 7 = 20
11 + 8 = 20

6) 9 + 8 = 18
19 – 18 = 1

2) 19 – 10 = 11
19 – 9 = 10

7) 18 + 2 = 20
18 – 12 = 10

3) 15 + 4 = 18
13 + 3 = 16

8) 11 + 6 = 16
11 – 5 = 6

4) 10 – 9 = 1
10 – 3 = 8

9) 14 + 6 = 19
19 – 6 = 13

5) 17 – 9 = 8
19 – 13 = 16

10) 15 + 3 = 17
15 + 4 = 19

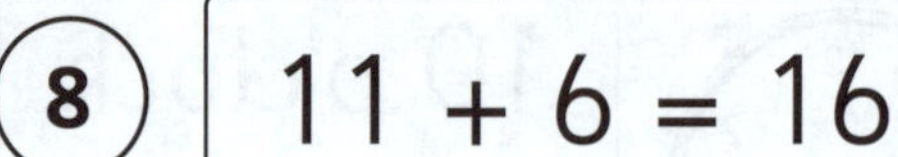

Today I scored ☐ out of 10.

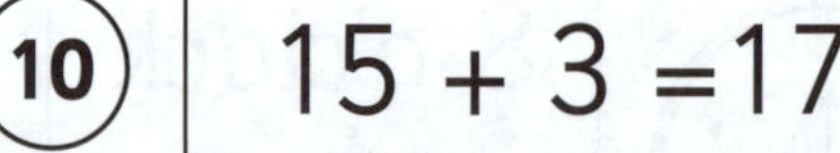

Year 1 Mental Maths — Summer Term

Week 9 — Day 1

1

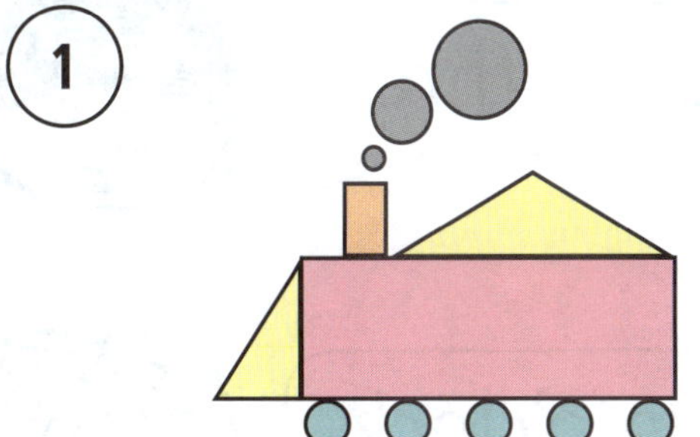

circles	rectangles
triangles	

2

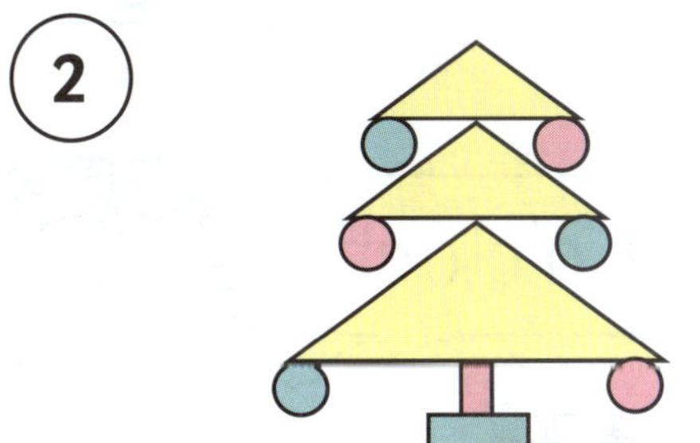

circles	rectangles
triangles	

3

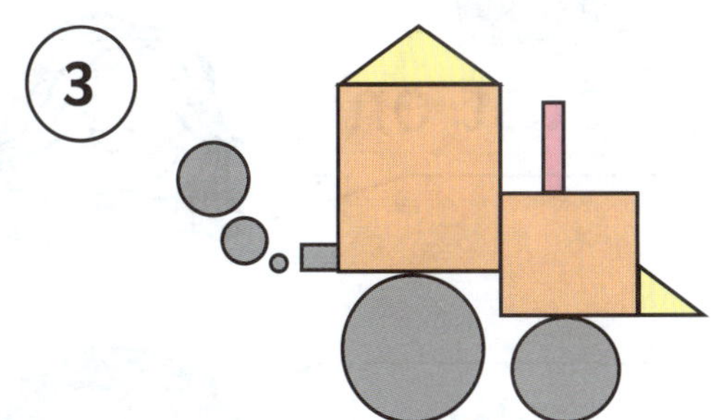

circles	rectangles
triangles	

4

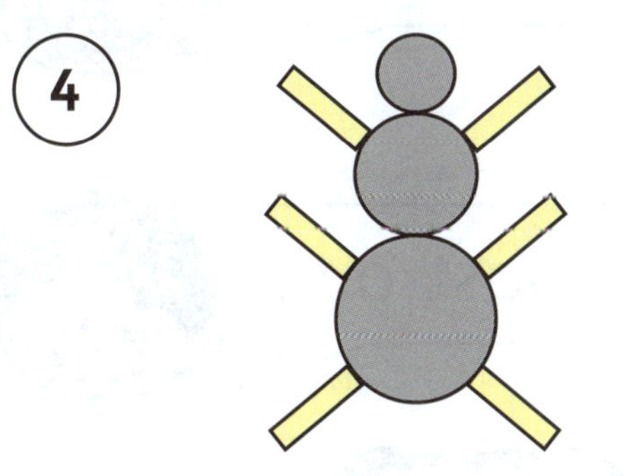

circles	rectangles
triangles	

Today I scored ☐ out of 4.

   Year 1 Mental Maths — Summer Term

Week 9 — Day 2

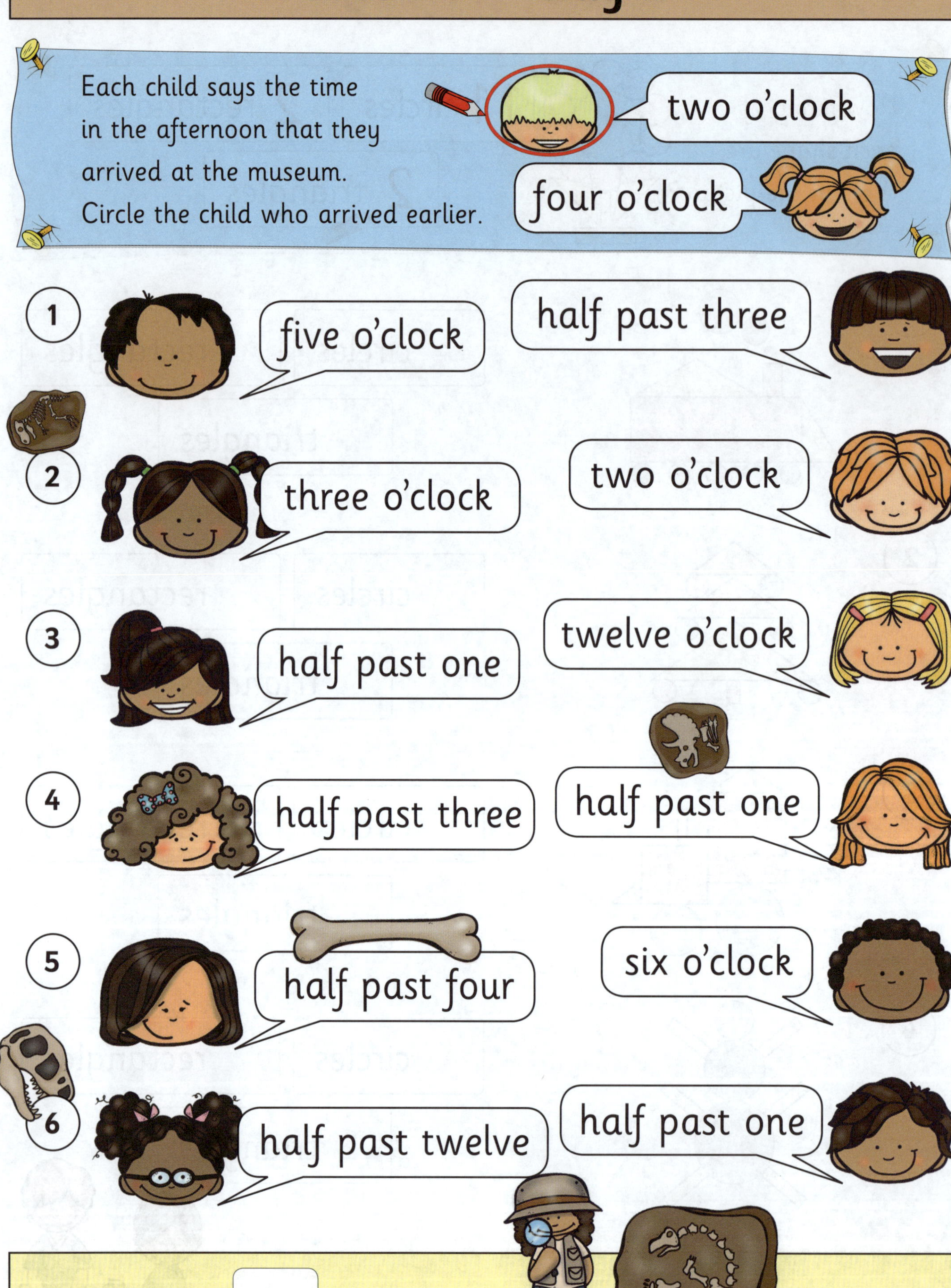

Each child says the time in the afternoon that they arrived at the museum.
Circle the child who arrived earlier.
two o'clock
four o'clock
1
five o'clock
half past three
2
three o'clock
two o'clock
3
half past one
twelve o'clock
4
half past three
half past one
5
half past four
six o'clock
6
half past twelve
half past one
Today I scored ___ out of 6.

Week 9 — Day 3

Write 'shorter' or 'longer' in the box to complete the sentence.

4 hours is **longer** than 2 hours.

1) 9 hours is __________ than 7 hours.

2) 5 hours is __________ than 10 hours.

3) 1 hour is __________ than 3 hours.

4) 7 hours is __________ than 1 hour.

5) 13 hours is __________ than 11 hours.

6) 16 hours is __________ than 18 hours.

7) 21 hours is __________ than 19 hours.

8) 22 hours is __________ than 27 hours.

Today I scored __________ out of 8.

Year 1 Mental Maths — Summer Term

Week 9 — Day 4

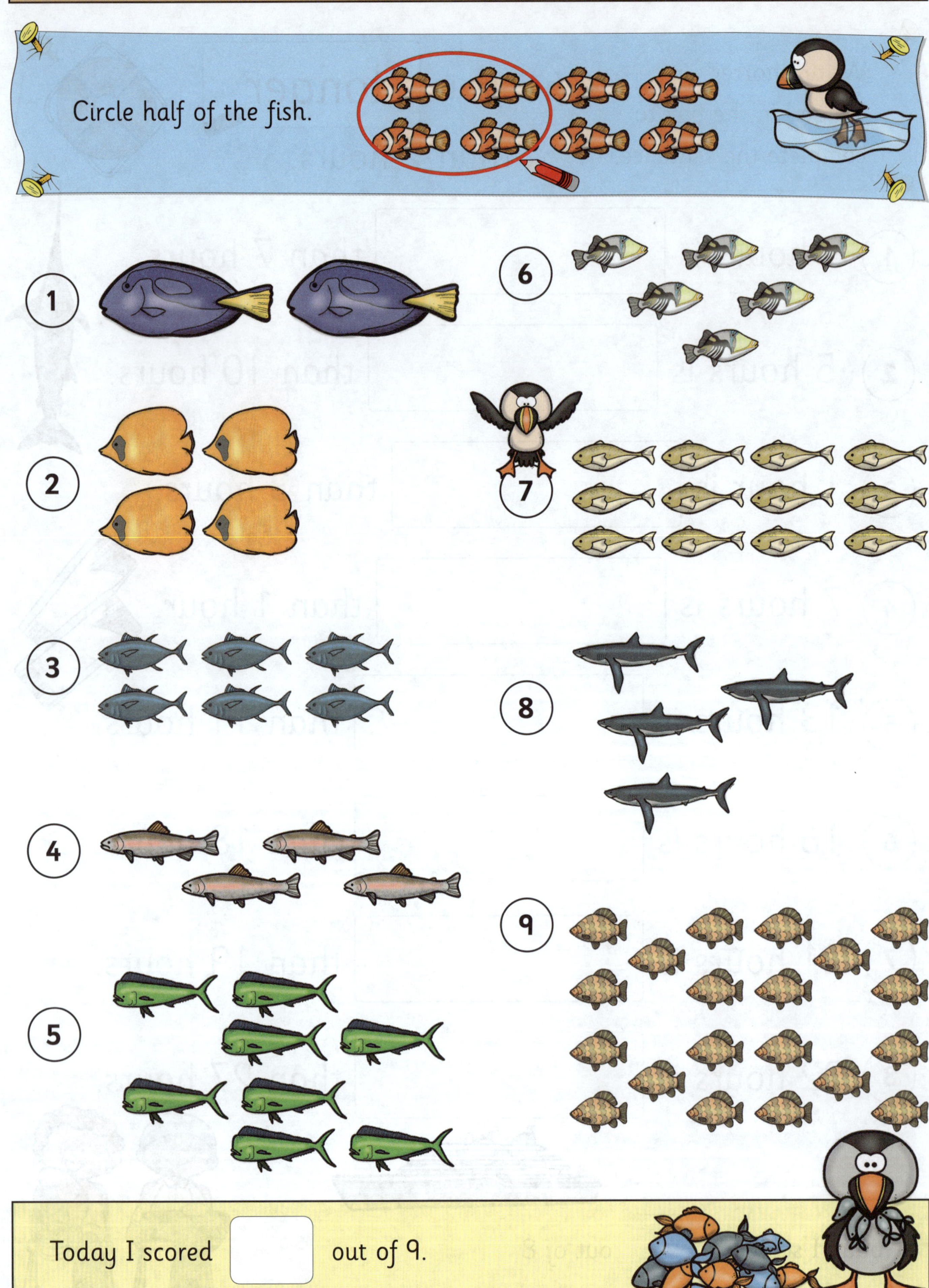

Circle half of the fish.

1

2

3

4

5

6

7

8

9

Today I scored ☐ out of 9.

Week 9 — Day 5

Write the answer to the calculation in words.

$4 + 13 =$ seventeen

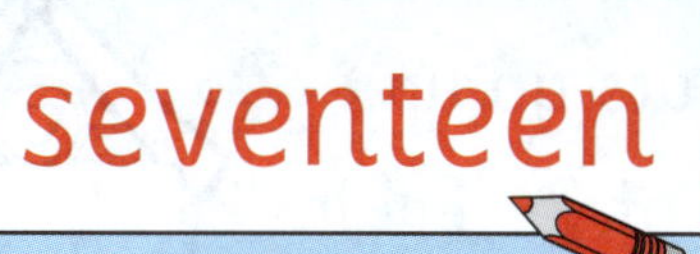

1. $9 + 7 =$

2. $17 - 5 =$

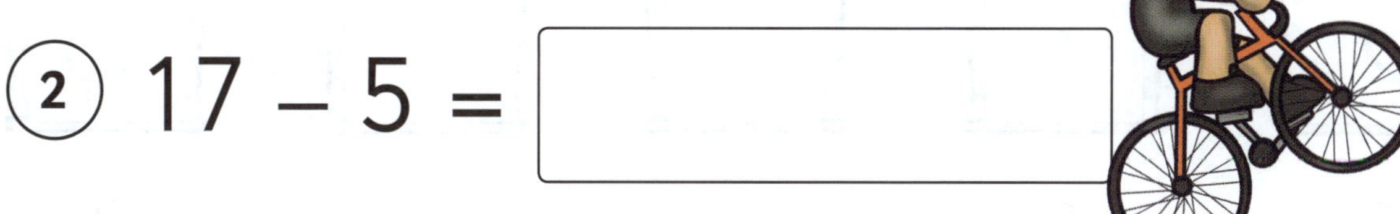

3. $10 + 4 =$

4. $8 + 11 =$

5. $20 - 16 =$

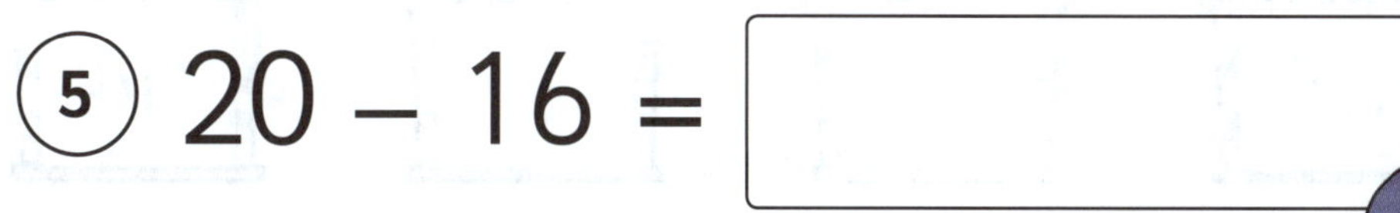

6. $18 - 12 =$

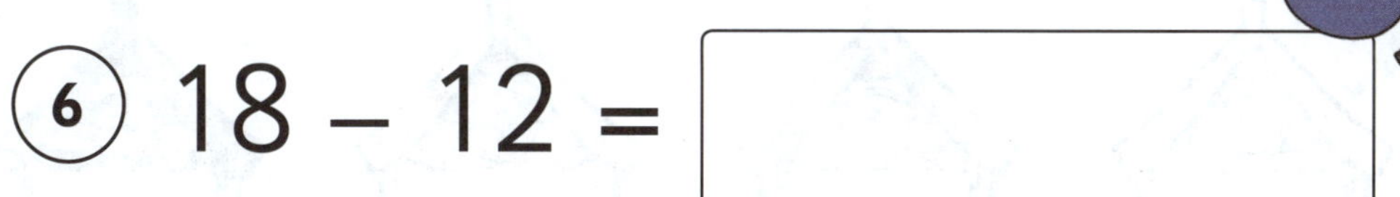

7. $16 + 3 =$

8. $13 - 7 =$

Today I scored ___ out of 8.

    Year 1 Mental Maths — Summer Term

Week 10 — Day 1

The numbers on the beach huts go up in steps of 2. Fill in the missing numbers.
16
18
20
22
1
2
4
10
2
34
36
38
3
86
88
94
4
50
54
56
5
70
72
74
Today I scored   out of 5.

Week 10 — Day 2

Dave delivers food. The table shows when he delivers different items. Complete the sentence.

Monday	bread
Tuesday	eggs
Wednesday	milk
Thursday	pies
Friday	cakes

Today is Tuesday. Tomorrow Dave will deliver

milk.

1 Today is Thursday.
Tomorrow Dave will deliver [ ].

2 Today is Wednesday.
Yesterday Dave delivered [ ].

3 Today is Friday.
Yesterday Dave delivered [ ].

4 Today is Tuesday.
In 2 days Dave will deliver [ ].

5 Today is Thursday.
2 days ago Dave delivered [ ].

6 Today is Monday.
In 2 days Dave will deliver [ ].

Today I scored [ ] out of 6.

Year 1 Mental Maths — Summer Term

Week 10 — Day 3

Fill in the gap in
the multiplication.
Use the pictures to help you.

$2 \times 5 = 10$

1 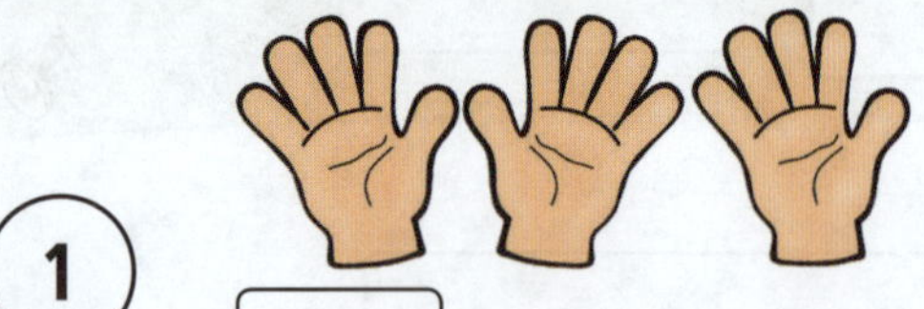

$\boxed{} \times 5 = 15$

5 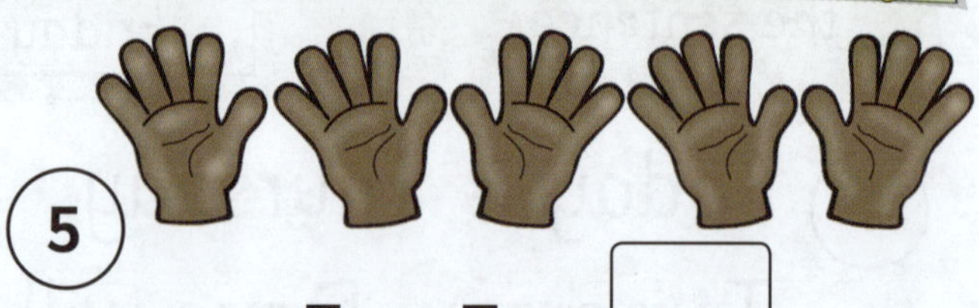

$5 \times 5 = \boxed{}$

2

$1 \times \boxed{} = 5$

6 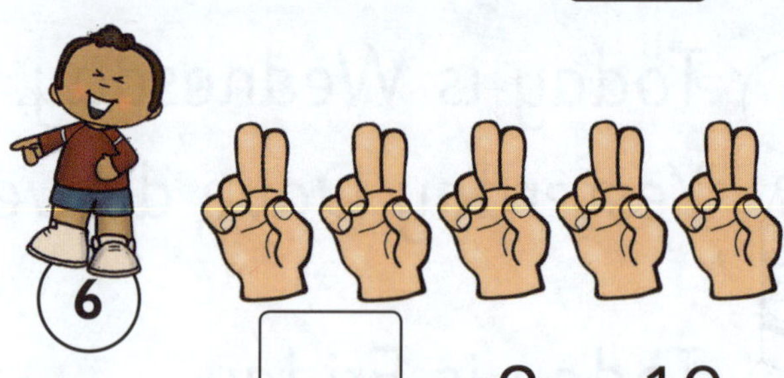

$\boxed{} \times 2 = 10$

3 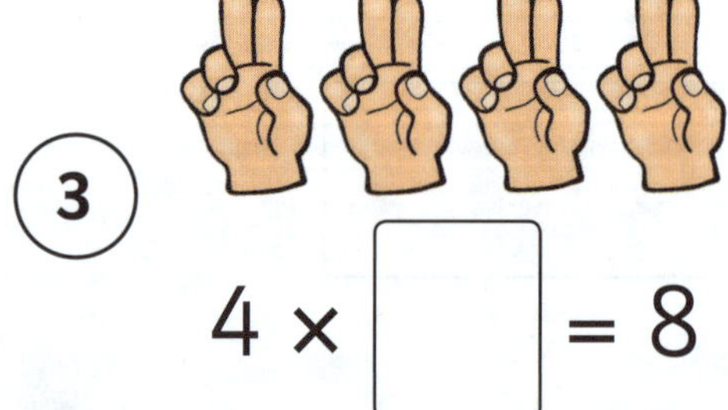

$4 \times \boxed{} = 8$

7 

$\boxed{} \times 5 = 20$

4 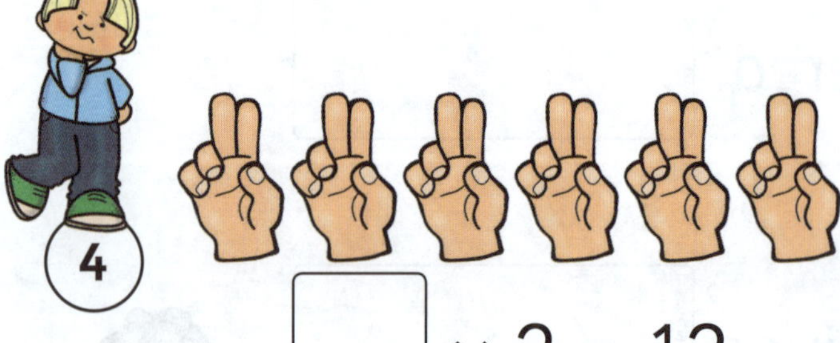

$\boxed{} \times 2 = 12$

8 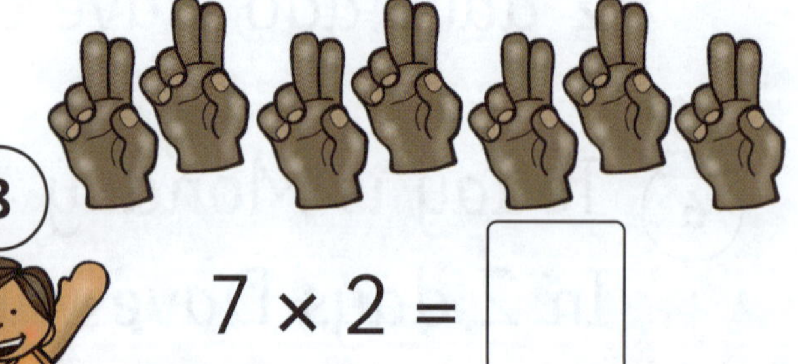

$7 \times 2 = \boxed{}$

Today I scored $\boxed{}$ out of 8.

Week 10 — Day 4

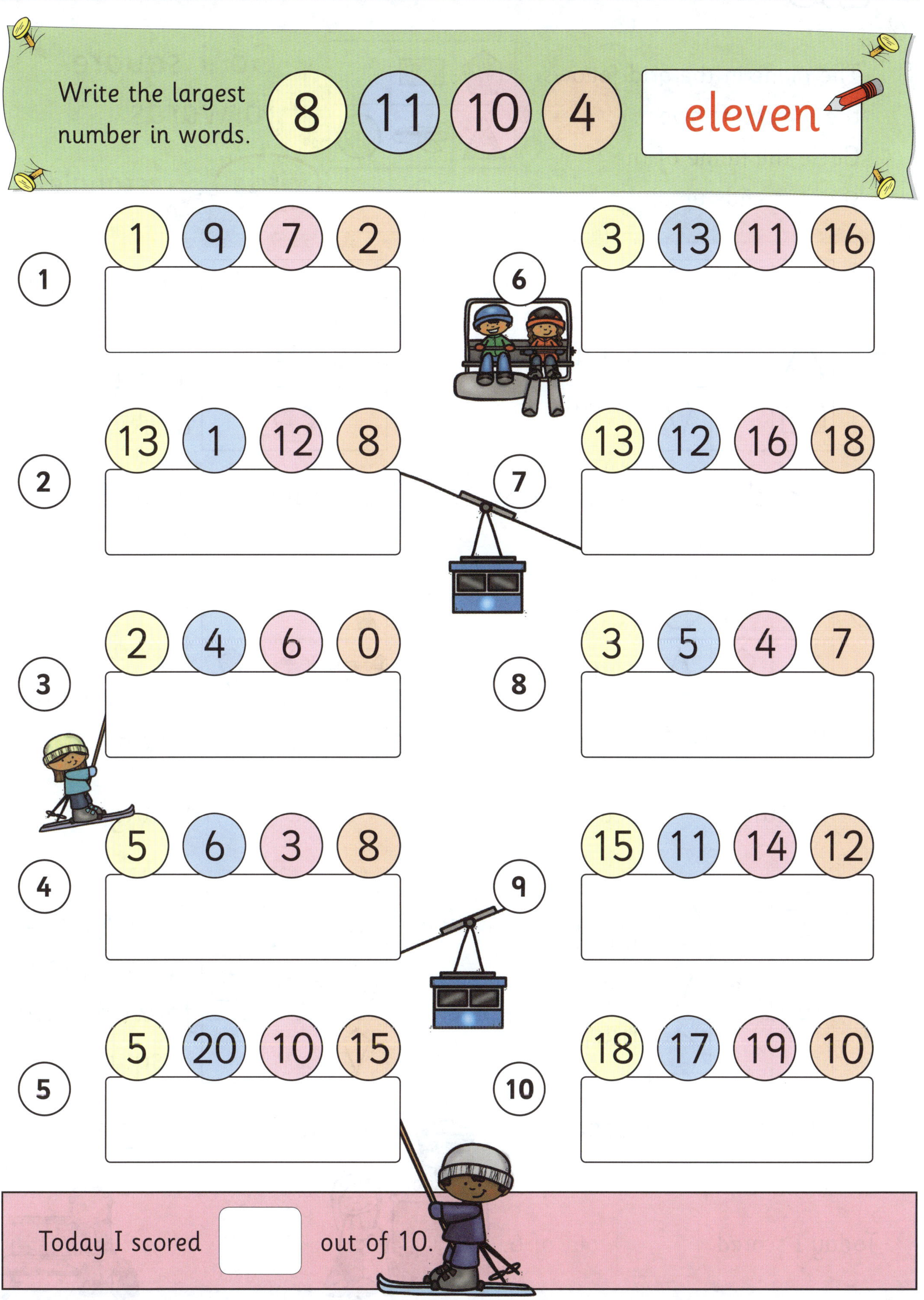

   Year 1 Mental Maths — Summer Term

Week 10 — Day 5

The plane in the grid follows the directions given. Circle the name of the shape it ends up on.

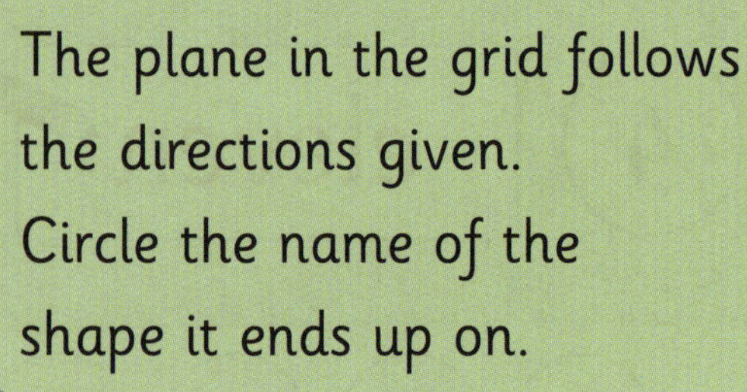

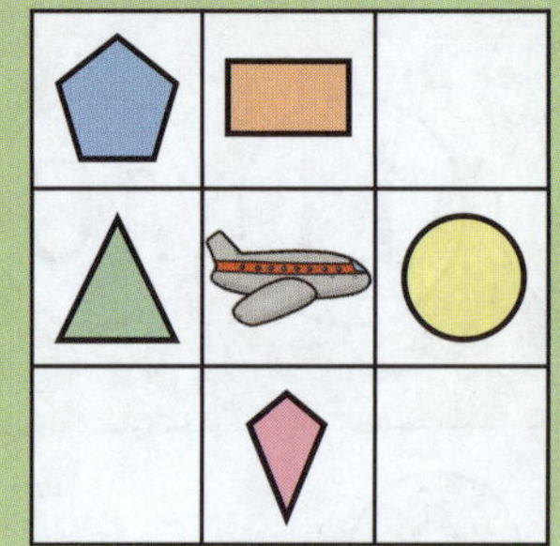
Go 1 square forwards.

circle   rectangle

1 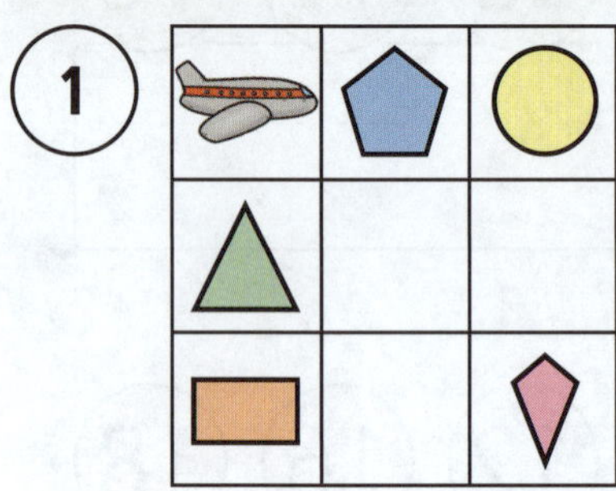 Go 2 squares down.

circle   rectangle

2 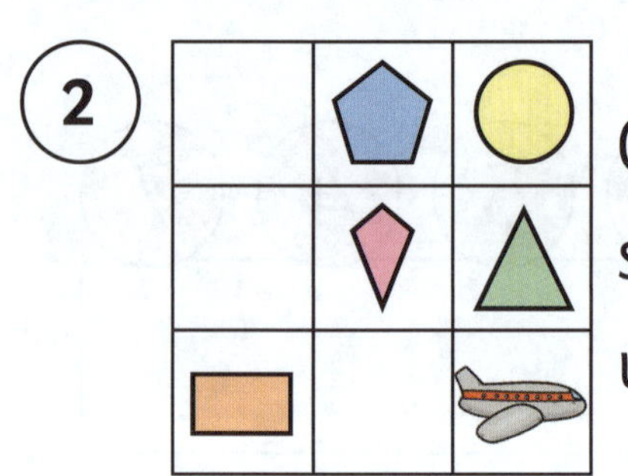 Go 2 squares up.

rectangle   circle

3  Go 1 square backwards.

triangle   rectangle

4 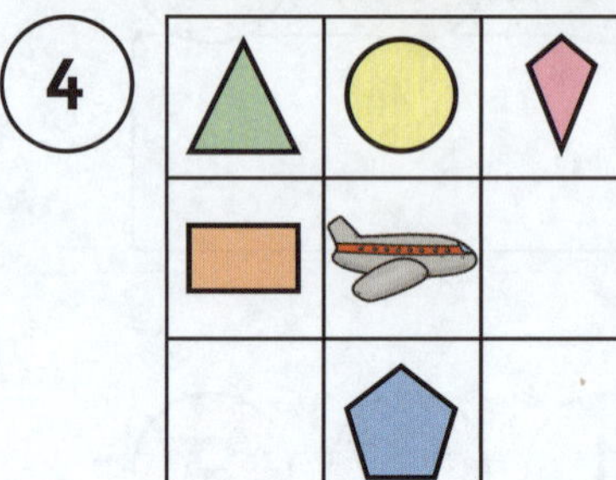 Go 1 square up, then 1 square backwards.

triangle   rectangle

5 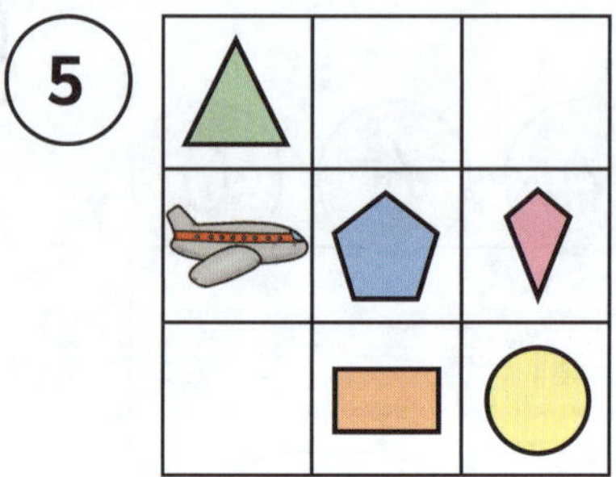 Go 2 squares forwards, then 1 square down.

circle   rectangle

6 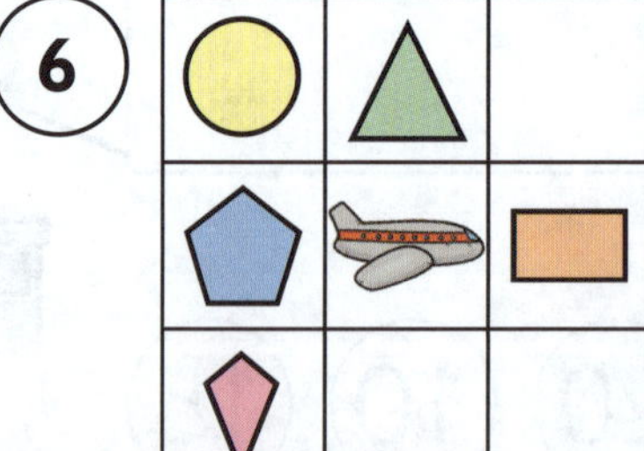 Go 1 square up, 1 square forwards, then 1 square down.

rectangle   triangle

Today I scored ☐ out of 6.

Week 11 — Day 1

Fill in the missing number.

$12 + 4 = \boxed{16}$

(1) $5 + 4 = \boxed{}$

(2) $6 + 0 = \boxed{}$

(3) $7 + 3 = \boxed{}$

(4) $13 + 4 = \boxed{}$

(5) $7 + \boxed{} = 10$

(6) $4 + \boxed{} = 15$

(7) $11 + 8 = \boxed{}$

(8) $12 + \boxed{} = 20$

(9) $\boxed{} + 9 = 9$

(10) $\boxed{} + 7 = 18$

Today I scored $\boxed{}$ out of 10.

Year 1 Mental Maths — Summer Term

Week 11 — Day 2

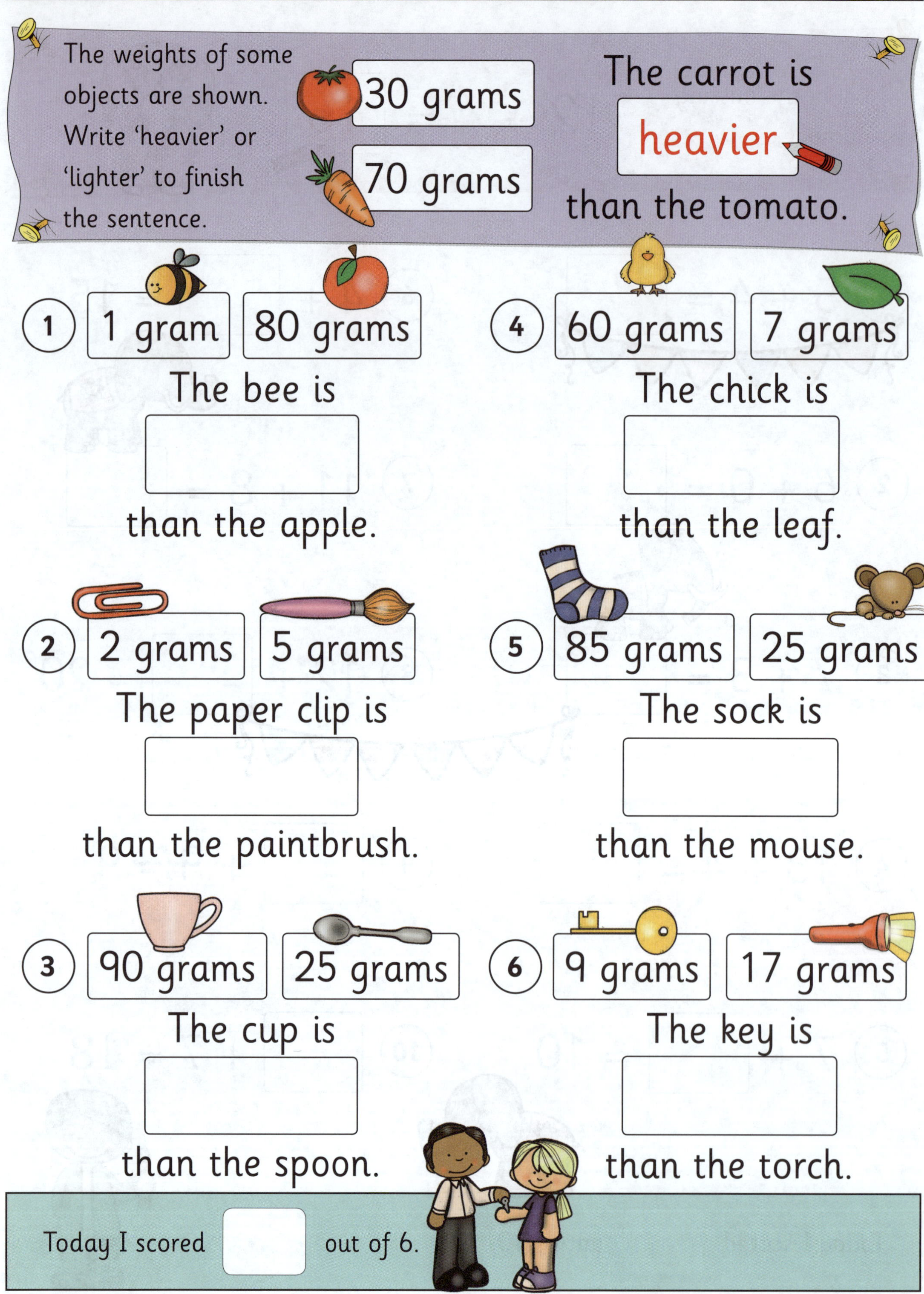

The weights of some objects are shown. Write 'heavier' or 'lighter' to finish the sentence.

30 grams
70 grams

The carrot is
heavier
than the tomato.

1   1 gram   80 grams
The bee is

than the apple.

2   2 grams   5 grams
The paper clip is

than the paintbrush.

3   90 grams   25 grams
The cup is

than the spoon.

4   60 grams   7 grams
The chick is

than the leaf.

5   85 grams   25 grams
The sock is

than the mouse.

6   9 grams   17 grams
The key is

than the torch.

Today I scored   out of 6.

Week 11 — Day 3

Is a half or a quarter of the shape shaded? Tick the right box.

☐ a quarter
☑ a half

1. ☐ a quarter ☐ a half

2. ☐ a quarter ☐ a half

3. ☐ a quarter ☐ a half

4. ☐ a quarter ☐ a half

5. ☐ a quarter ☐ a half

6. ☐ a quarter ☐ a half

7. ☐ a quarter ☐ a half

8. ☐ a quarter ☐ a half

9. ☐ a quarter ☐ a half

10. ☐ a quarter ☐ a half

Today I scored ☐ out of 10.

Year 1 Mental Maths — Summer Term

Week 11 — Day 4

1

under | on top of

4

under | on top of

2

under | on top of

5

under | on top of

3

under | on top of

6

under | on top of

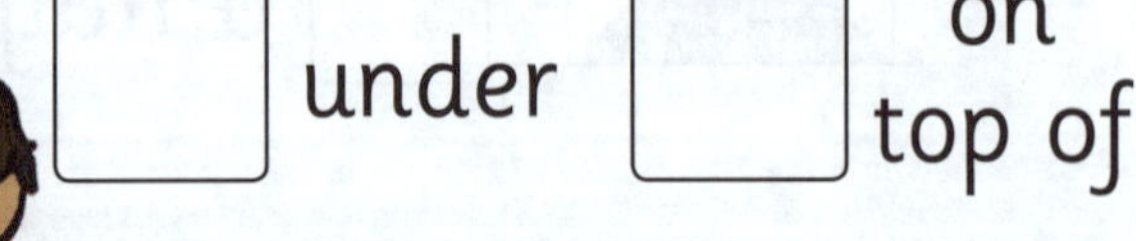

Today I scored [ ] out of 6.

Week 11 — Day 5

Write + or − to finish the number sentence.

$1 \; \boxed{+} \; 7 = 8$

1. $6 \; \boxed{} \; 3 = 9$

2. $14 \; \boxed{} \; 5 = 9$

3. $8 \; \boxed{} \; 2 = 6$

4. $2 \; \boxed{} \; 5 = 7$

5. $4 = 9 \; \boxed{} \; 5$

6. $19 = 14 \; \boxed{} \; 5$

7. $12 \; \boxed{} \; 3 = 15$

8. $20 = 12 \; \boxed{} \; 8$

9. $8 = 17 \; \boxed{} \; 9$

10. $14 = 6 \; \boxed{} \; 8$

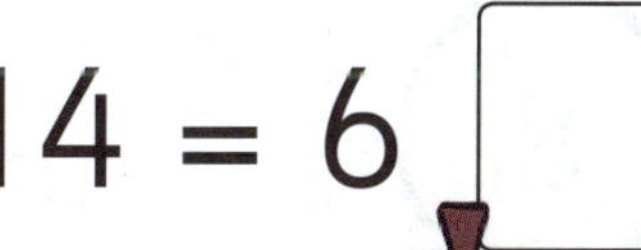

Today I scored $\boxed{}$ out of 10.

Year 1 Mental Maths — Summer Term

Week 12 — Day 1

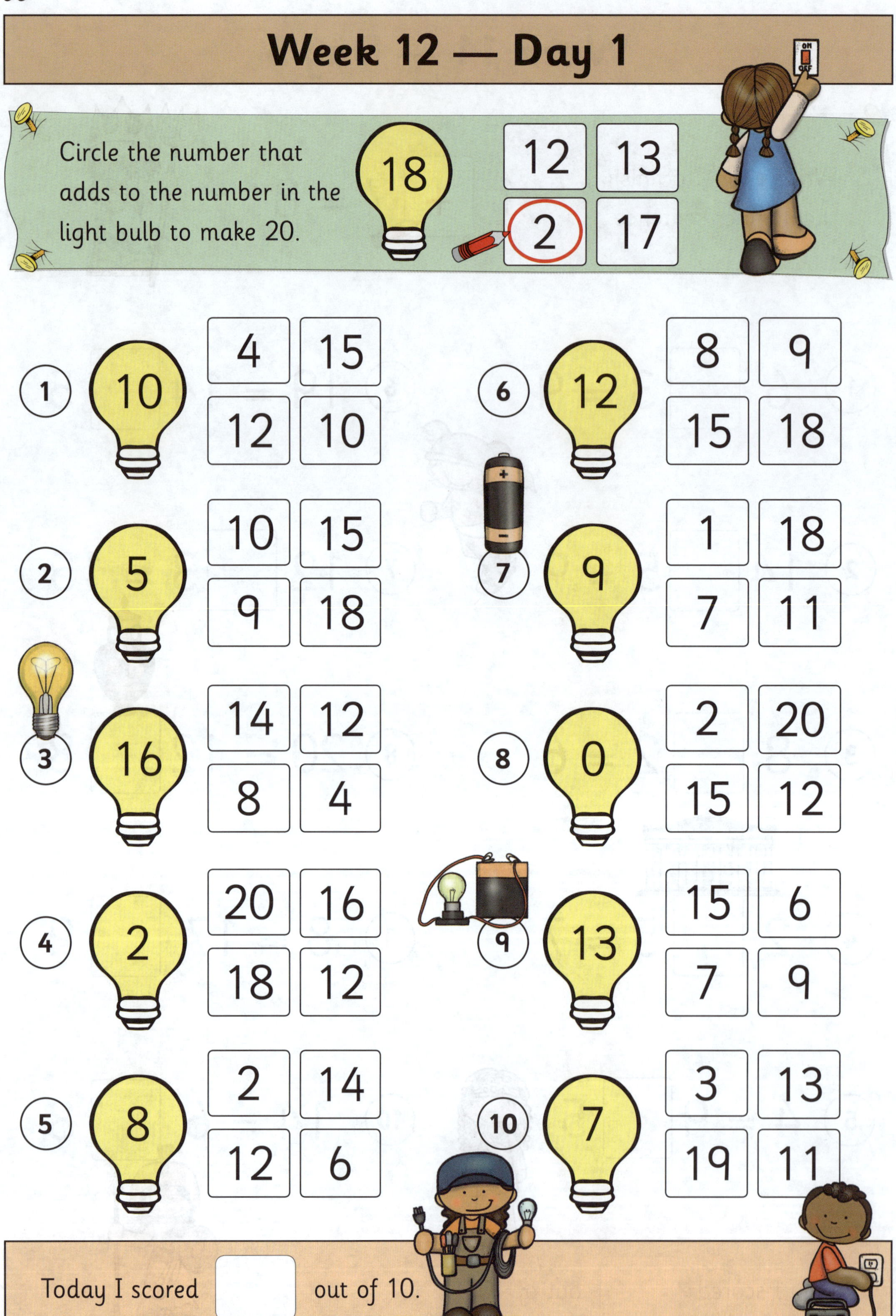

Circle the number that adds to the number in the light bulb to make 20.

Today I scored ☐ out of 10.

Week 12 — Day 2

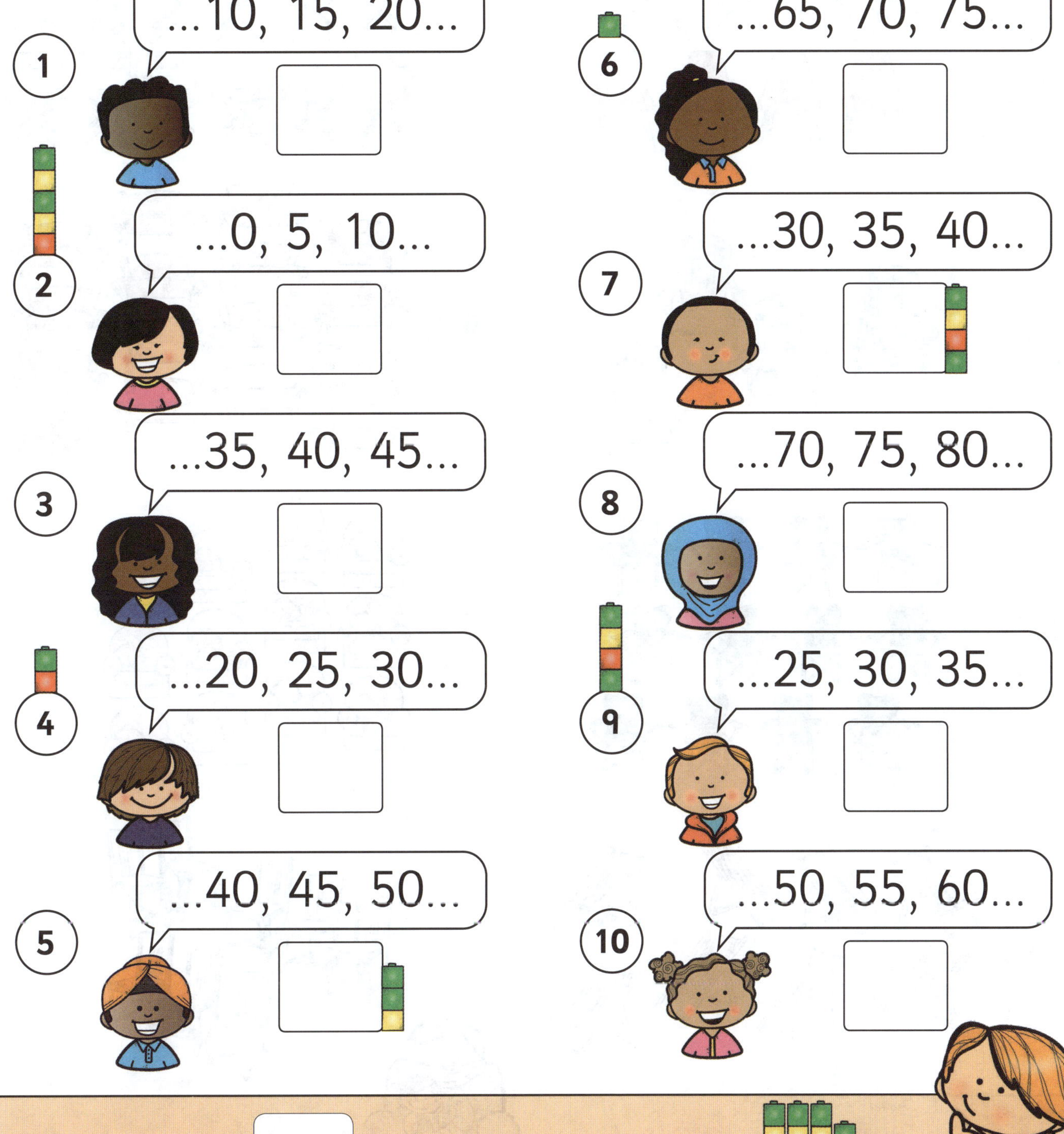

Year 1 Mental Maths — Summer Term

Week 12 — Day 3

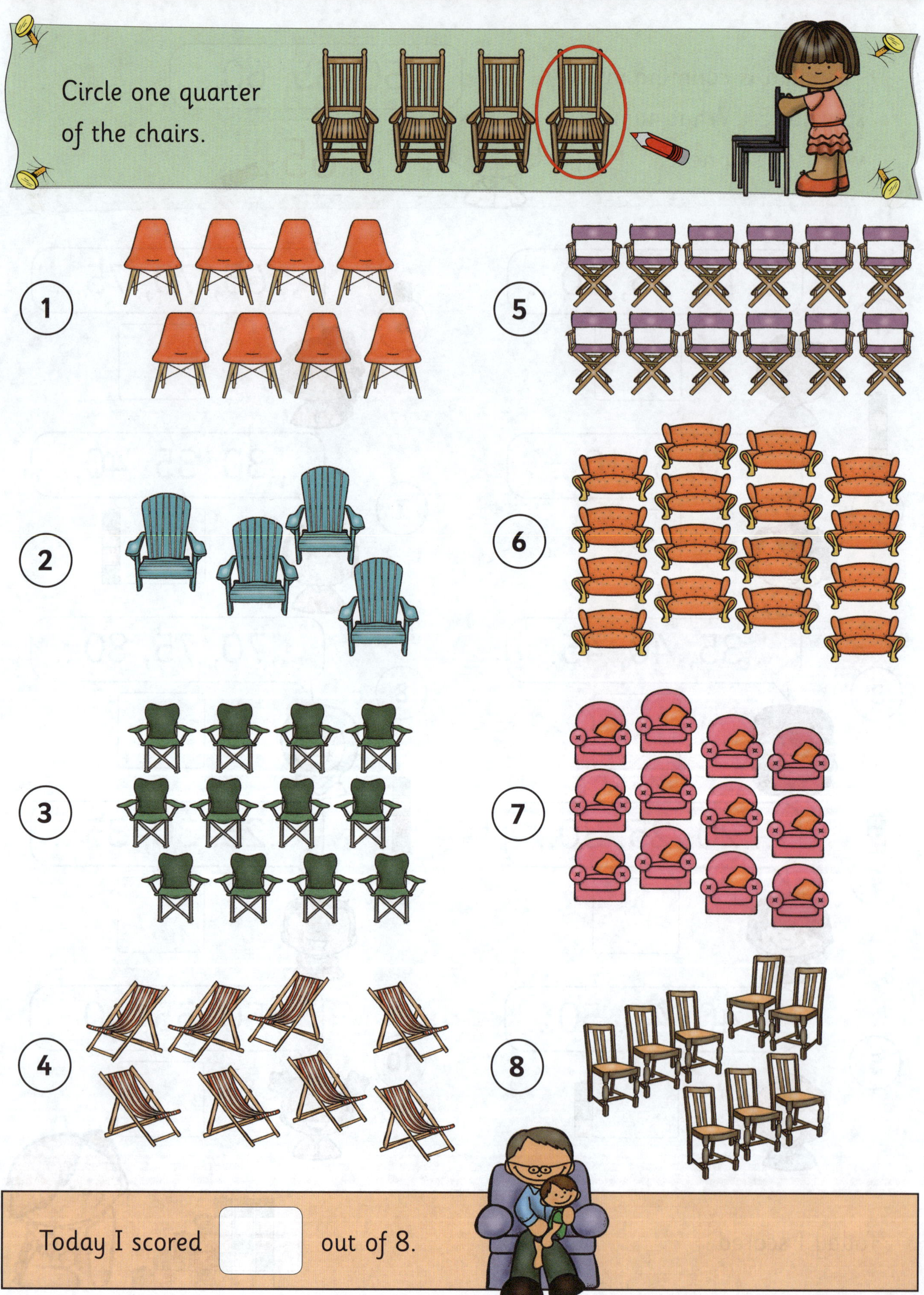

Today I scored ☐ out of 8.

Week 12 — Day 4

The seeds are shared equally between the pots. How many seeds will there be in each pot?

1 each

1  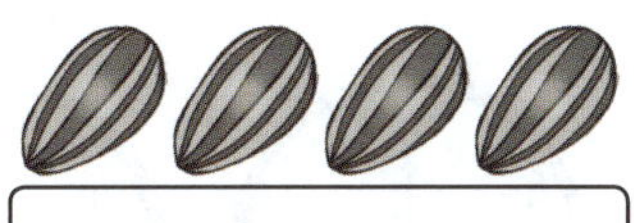 [ ] each

5   [ ] each

2   [ ] each

6   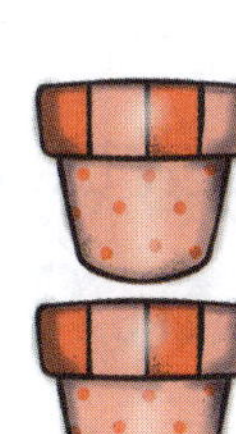 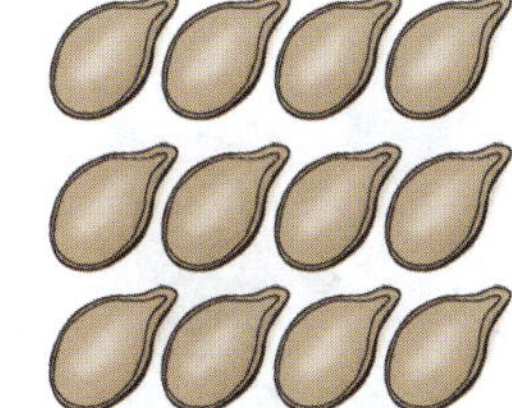 [ ] each

3    [ ] each

7  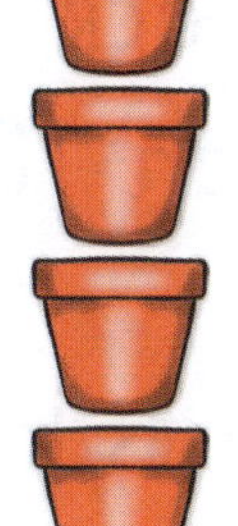  [ ] each

4   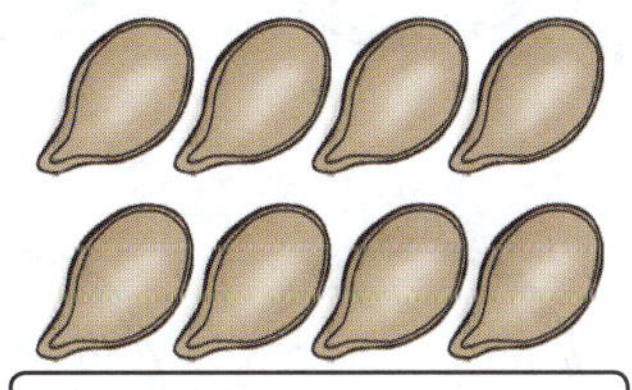 [ ] each

8    [ ] each

Today I scored [ ] out of 8.

     Year 1 Mental Maths — Summer Term

Week 12 — Day 5

It is sports day. Circle the clock that shows when the race could start.

1.  starts later than 10 o'clock 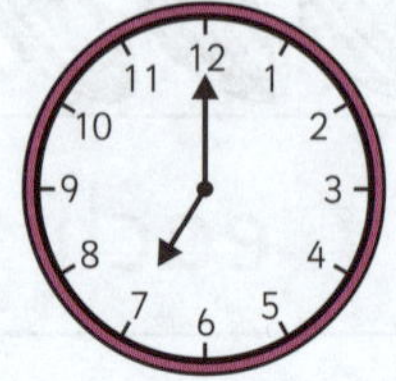  

2.  starts earlier than 9 o'clock 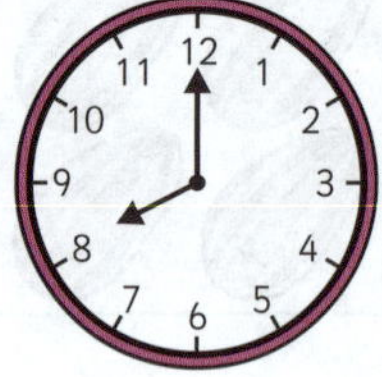  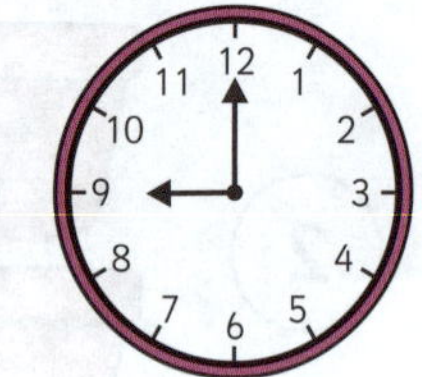

3.  starts later than 9 o'clock and earlier than 10 o'clock   

4.  starts later than 10 o'clock and earlier than 11 o'clock   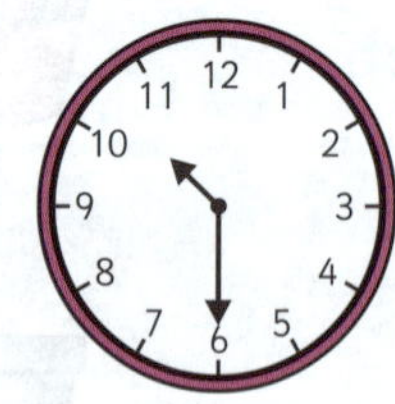

5.  starts later than half past 11   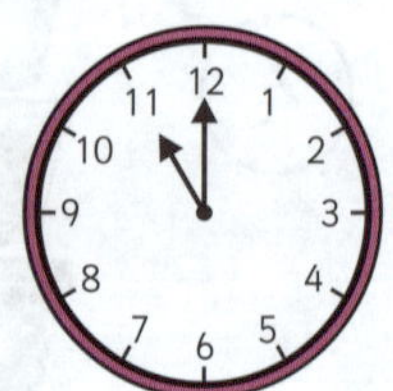

Today I scored ☐ out of 5.

Answers

Week 1 — Day 1

1. 15
2. 17
3. 13
4. 10
5. 1
6. 6
7. 2
8. 11

Week 1 — Day 2

1. 4
2. 8
3. 2
4. 10
5. 20
6. 12
7. 14
8. 16

Week 1 — Day 3

1. 60
2. 14
3. 35
4. 30
5. 3

Week 1 — Day 4

1. 20 grams
2. 40 grams
3. 50 grams
4. 40 grams
5. 30 grams
6. 50 grams

Week 1 — Day 5

1. 4
2. 3
3. 5
4. 6
5. 9

Week 2 — Day 1

1. 4
2. 1
3. 3
4. 5
5. 8
6. 10

Week 2 — Day 2

1. triangle
2. rectangle
3. circle
4. triangle
5. rectangle

Week 2 — Day 3

1. 6
2. 2
3. 12
4. 8
5. 4
6. 20
7. 16
8. 14

Week 2 — Day 4

1. **4 ÷ 2 = 2**
2. **2 ÷ 2 = 1**
3. **10 ÷ 2 = 5**
4. **14 ÷ 2 = 7**

Week 2 — Day 5

1. 6
2. 4
3. 1
4. 8
5. 6
6. 19
7. 20
8. 11
9. 18
10. 11

Week 3 — Day 1

1. 90, 100
2. 30, 36
3. 35, 45
4. 2, 4
5. 20, 30

Week 3 — Day 2

1. 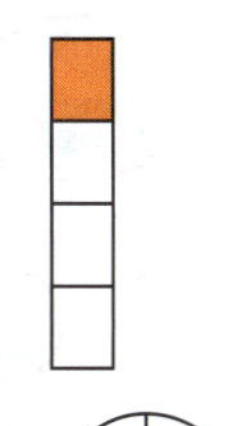
2. 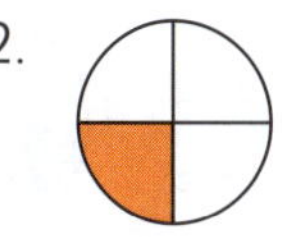
3. 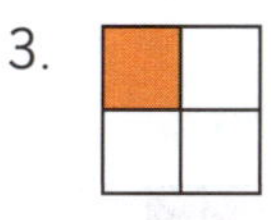
4. 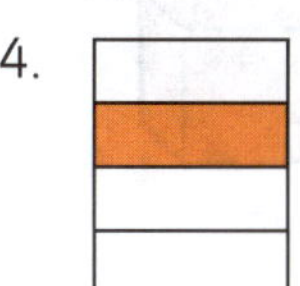
5. 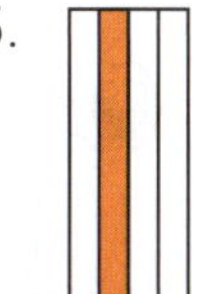
6. 
7. 
8. 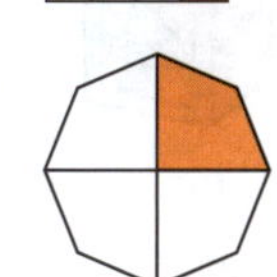

Week 3 — Day 3

1. 5
2. 2
3. 2
4. 2
5. 5
6. 5
7. 2

Week 3 — Day 4

1. 2
2. 4
3. 1
4. 6
5. 5
6. 7
7. 8
8. 9

Week 3 — Day 5

1. 10
2. 6
3. 3
4. 2
5. 6
6. 5
7. 8
8. 14
9. 13
10. 12

Week 4 — Day 1

1. cube
2. cuboid
3. cube
4. pyramid
5. sphere
6. sphere

Week 4 — Day 2

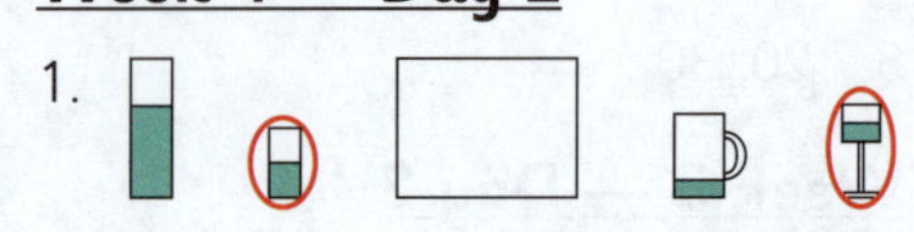

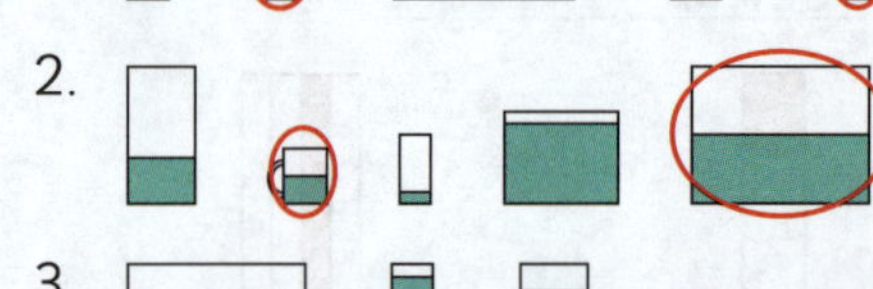

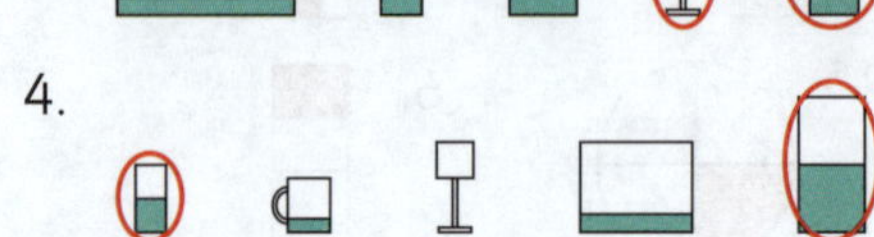

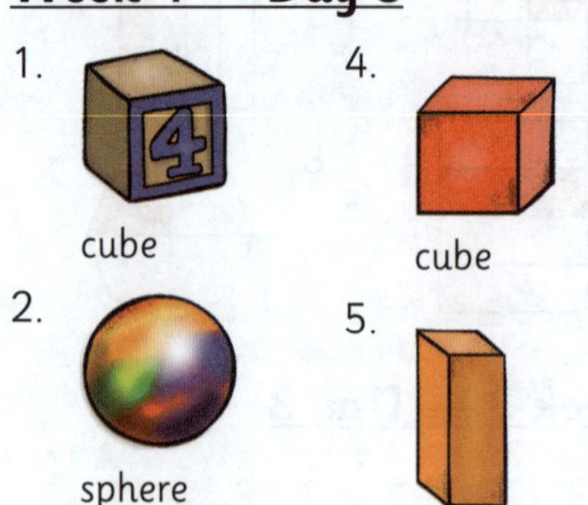

Week 4 — Day 3

1. 
   cube
2. sphere
3. cuboid
4. cube
5. cuboid

Week 4 — Day 4

1. 8 litres
2. 6 litres
3. 2 litres
4. 4 litres
5. 14 litres
6. 18 litres
7. 16 litres
8. 20 litres

Week 4 — Day 5

1. 4 and 2
2. 1 and 7
3. 6 and 1
4. 1 and 10
5. 12 and 15
6. 6 and 16
7. 16 and 4
8. 8 and 16
9. 6 and 13
10. 1 and 19

Week 5 — Day 1

1. 1 above
   4 below
2. 4 above
   5 below
3. 0 above
   2 below
4. 2 above
   7 below
5. 7 above
   5 below

Week 5 — Day 2

1. 9 – 3
2. 11 – 2
3. 2 + 5
4. 9 + 6
5. 5 + 5
6. 9 + 9
7. 6 + 7
8. 16 – 11

Week 5 — Day 3

1. 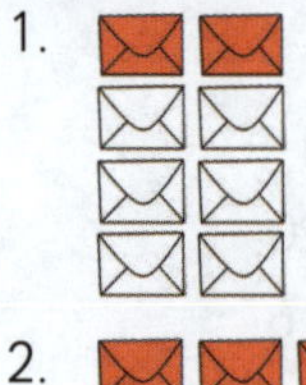
2. 
3. 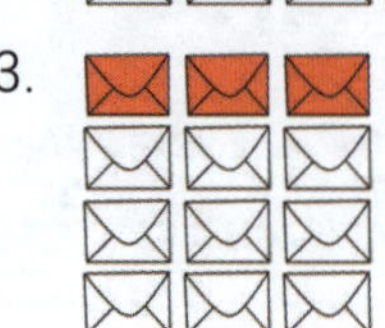
4. 
5. 

Week 5 — Day 4

1. 4
2. 6
3. 1
4. 6
5. 2
6. 6
7. 8
8. 8

Week 5 — Day 5

1. six
2. five
3. nine
4. fourteen
5. twelve
6. seventeen
7. eleven
8. nineteen

Week 6 — Day 1

Week 6 — Day 2

1. S
2. E
3. E
4. W
5. S
6. N
7. E
8. N

Week 6 — Day 3

1. 3
2. 1
3. 7
4. 6
5. 10
6. 7
7. 8
8. 12
9. 9
10. 11

Week 6 — Day 4

1. 4
2. 3
3. 12
4. 3
5. 16
6. 5

Week 6 — Day 5

1. 6 cm
2. 2 cm
3. 8 cm
4. 10 cm
5. 12 cm
6. 16 cm
7. 14 cm

Week 7 — Day 1

1. 10, 30
2. 40, 50
3. 0, 40
4. 50, 60
5. 70, 90

Week 7 — Day 2

1. 40 g
2. 80 g
3. 30 g
4. 20 g
5. 100 g
6. 50 g
7. 10 g
8. 70 g

Week 7 — Day 3

1. March
2. Saturday
3. September
4. Tuesday
5. July
6. Tuesday
7. June
8. Saturday

Week 7 — Day 4

1. 20p, 10p
2. 50p, £1
3. 20p, 50p
4. 5p, 20p
5. 20p, 50p

Week 7 — Day 5

1. 5
2. 14
3. 13
4. 10
5. 17
6. 1
7. 8
8. 18

Week 8 — Day 1

1. 7
2. 10
3. 9
4. 11
5. 14

Week 8 — Day 2

1. Yes
2. No
3. No
4. Yes
5. Yes
6. No

Week 8 — Day 3

1. 5
2. 15
3. 10
4. 25
5. 35

Week 8 — Day 4

1. 9 o'clock
2. 5 o'clock
3. 11 o'clock
4. 2 o'clock
5. 10 o'clock
6. half past 4
7. half past 9
8. half past 12
9. half past 2
10. half past 6

Week 8 — Day 5

1. $13 + 7 = 20$
2. $19 - 9 = 10$
3. $13 + 3 = 16$
4. $10 - 9 = 1$
5. $17 - 9 = 8$
6. $19 - 18 = 1$
7. $18 + 2 = 20$
8. $11 - 5 = 6$
9. $19 - 6 = 13$
10. $15 + 4 = 19$

Week 9 — Day 1

1. 8 circles
   2 rectangles
   2 triangles
2. 6 circles
   2 rectangles
   3 triangles
3. 5 circles
   4 rectangles
   2 triangles
4. 3 circles
   6 rectangles
   0 triangles

Week 9 — Day 2

1. 
2.
3.
4. 
5.
6.

Week 9 — Day 3

1. longer
2. shorter
3. shorter
4. longer
5. longer
6. shorter
7. longer
8. shorter

Week 9 — Day 4

1. 1 fish circled
2. 2 fish circled
3. 3 fish circled
4. 2 fish circled
5. 4 fish circled
6. 3 fish circled
7. 6 fish circled
8. 2 fish circled
9. 10 fish circled

Week 9 — Day 5

1. sixteen
2. twelve
3. fourteen
4. nineteen
5. four
6. six
7. nineteen
8. six

Week 10 — Day 1

1. 6, 8
2. 40, 42
3. 90, 92
4. 48, 52
5. 66, 68

Week 10 — Day 2

1. cakes
2. eggs
3. pies
4. pies
5. eggs
6. milk

Week 10 — Day 3

1. 3
2. 5
3. 2
4. 6
5. 25
6. 5
7. 4
8. 14

Week 10 — Day 4

1. nine
2. thirteen
3. six
4. eight
5. twenty
6. sixteen
7. eighteen
8. seven
9. fifteen
10. nineteen

Week 10 — Day 5

1. rectangle
2. circle
3. triangle
4. triangle
5. circle
6. rectangle

Week 11 — Day 1

1. 9
2. 6
3. 10
4. 17
5. 3
6. 11
7. 19
8. 8
9. 0
10. 11

Week 11 — Day 2

1. lighter
2. lighter
3. heavier
4. heavier
5. heavier
6. lighter

Week 11 — Day 3

1. a quarter
2. a quarter
3. a half
4. a half
5. a quarter
6. a quarter
7. a half
8. a half
9. a half
10. a quarter

Week 11 — Day 4

1. 2 under, 2 on top of
2. 4 under, 1 on top of
3. 3 under, 4 on top of
4. 6 under, 3 on top of
5. 4 under, 6 on top of
6. 5 under, 7 on top of

Week 11 — Day 5

1. +
2. −
3. −
4. +
5. −
6. +
7. +
8. +
9. −
10. +

Week 12 — Day 1

1. 10
2. 15
3. 4
4. 18
5. 12
6. 8
7. 11
8. 20
9. 7
10. 13

Week 12 — Day 2

1. 25
2. 15
3. 50
4. 35
5. 55
6. 80
7. 45
8. 85
9. 40
10. 65

Week 12 — Day 3

1. 2 chairs circled
2. 1 chair circled
3. 3 chairs circled
4. 2 chairs circled
5. 3 chairs circled
6. 4 chairs circled
7. 3 chairs circled
8. 2 chairs circled

Week 12 — Day 4

1. 2
2. 3
3. 4
4. 2
5. 5
6. 6
7. 3
8. 4

Week 12 — Day 5

1. 

2. 

3. 

4. 

5. 

M1MWSU11